The American Journalists

THE POLITICAL ACTIVITIES
OF PHILIP FRENEAU

Samuel E. Forman

ARNO
&
The New York Times

Collection Created and Selected
by Charles Gregg of Gregg Press

Reprint edition 1970 by Arno Press Inc.

LC# 77-125693
ISBN 0-405-01670-0

The American Journalists
ISBN for complete set: 0-405-01650-6

Reprinted from a copy in
The Columbia University Library

Manufactured in the United States of America

THE POLITICAL ACTIVITIES OF
PHILIP FRENEAU

SERIES XX   NOS. 9-10

JOHNS HOPKINS UNIVERSITY STUDIES

IN

HISTORICAL AND POLITICAL SCIENCE

(Edited 1882-1901 by H. B. ADAMS.)

J. M. VINCENT

J. H. HOLLANDER   W. W. WILLOUGHBY

Editors

———

THE POLITICAL ACTIVITIES OF PHILIP FRENEAU

BY

SAMUEL E. FORMAN, Ph. D.

———

BALTIMORE

THE JOHNS HOPKINS PRESS

PUBLISHED MONTHLY

SEPTEMBER-OCTOBER, 1902

The Lord Baltimore Press
THE FRIEDENWALD COMPANY
BALTIMORE, MD.

PREFACE

In this sketch of Philip Freneau I have tried to bring out in its proper proportion the public side of the man's career. There have appeared several accounts of Freneau as a poet, and these are appreciative and just. But as a politician and publicist Freneau has not received the attention which he deserves. Historians have been content to bestow upon him a contemptuous phrase and let him pass. He is a "reptile journalist," a "barking cur," a "low editor," a "democratic scribbler." Such treatment is unfair to the memory of Freneau and is not good history. Any one who will take the trouble to get at the facts of Freneau's life will find that he deserves the gratitude of posterity, not its contempt. It was a long and stormy life and it was lived for human rights and human freedom.

In the prosecution of my work I have been greatly assisted by the Librarians of the New York Historical Society and of the Pennsylvania Historical Society, and to these gentlemen my thanks are due. I am also indebted to the late Professor H. B. Adams and to Dr. J. M. Vincent, of the Johns Hopkins University, for valuable suggestions.

S. E. FORMAN.

CONTENTS

THE POLITICAL ACTIVITIES OF PHILIP FRENEAU

CHAPTER I

YOUTH AND EARLY MANHOOD

Philip Freneau was born of Huguenot parentage in the city of New York, January 13, 1752. His father died when Philip was but a child. His mother upon the death of her husband removed from New York to New Jersey, and with her four children established herself upon the Freneau estate of Mount Pleasant, a settlement just outside of Middletown Point (now Mattawan) in Monmouth county. Philip was given into the hands of good tutors and proved to be a diligent pupil. One of his teachers was the Rev. William Tennant, a divine whose name is still held in blessed memory in Monmouth county. Dr. Tennant was acting president of Princeton College when Freneau entered that institution as a Freshman in 1767.[1] The youth was so well prepared that the president wrote a note to Mrs. Freneau congratulating her upon her son's superior acquirements.[2] Philip remained at Princeton College for four years, and during that period his future career was largely determined. The college was a hot-bed of whiggism.[3] Teachers and students joined in resisting the

[1] Hageman's History of the College of New Jersey.
[2] Griswold's Poets of America, p. 31.
[3] " Several years before a speck of war against the mother country could be discovered, an electric spark of patriotic fire was struck in Princeton which betokened the flame that afterward lighted up New Jersey. James Madison in 1770 wrote to Thomas

pretensions and aggressions of England. The president, John Witherspoon, was one of the signers of the Declaration of Independence. Among the students in whose minds rebellion was germinating were Henry Lee, Hugh Brackenridge, Samuel Spring, William Bradford, Aaron Burr, Frederick Frelinghuysen and James Madison.[4] With these great spirits Freneau mingled freely. James Madison was his classmate, while Brackenridge, Madison and Freneau formed a friendship which remained firm not only during their college career, but which was dissolved in after years only by death. "These three," says Griswold, "were all gifted with satirical powers which they were fond of displaying as frequently as there were occasions. They joined in lampooning not only the leaders of adverse parties in college, but also those prominent public characters who opposed the growing enthusiasm of the people for liberty. I have before me a considerable manuscript volume of personal and political satires written by them in about equal proportions."[5] Freneau and Brackenridge tried their hands at verse as well. In the attempt Brackenridge discovered what he could not do, although vanity constrained him to an occasional indulgence in bad verse all his life. Freneau's sophomoric pen, on the other hand, moved easily and gracefully and turned off lines that sometimes sparkled with the light of genius. Some of these youthful pieces were included by Freneau in an edition of his poems published in after years. Most of them are of no consequence, yet they show that Freneau's native talent for verse writing was very strong.

Martin: 'We have no news but the base conduct of the merchants in breaking through the spirited resolutions not to import. The letters to the merchants regarding their concurrence were lately burned by the students of this place in the college yard, all of them appearing in black gowns and the bell tolling. There are about 115 in the college grammar school, all of them in American cloth.' " Princeton and its Institutions, vol. i, p. 101.

[4] MacLean's History of the College of New Jersey.

[5] Poets of America, p. 14.

Freneau was graduated in distinguished company in 1771. It is doubtful whether Princeton College has ever sent out a class that contained a larger per cent of celebrated men. Of the eight who then took their degrees, six achieved fame and high position in church, in state, in letters, and in science,[*] yet neither Freneau nor Madison, apparently, took any of the prizes. In the records of the college there is an account of the commencement exercises of 1771, and the sixth and seventh items of the programme are as follows:

6. An English forensic dispute on the question: Does Ancient poetry excel Modern? Mr. Freneau the respondent, being necessarily absent, his argument in favor of the ancients was read. Mr. Williamson answered him; Mr. McKnight replied.

7. A poem on "The Rising Glory of America" by Mr. Brackenridge, was received with great applause.[†]

A little further ·down in the account we find that Mr. Madison was also excused from attending the exercises. One would like to know where those two young gentlemen were upon this important occasion. Freneau ought certainly to have been present for he was the largest contributor to the entertainment. In addition to his speech on the poetry of the ancients, he was the principal author of the poem that was read by Mr. Brackenridge and that gained such hearty applause. There can be no doubt that this poem was for the most part composed by Freneau, for Brackenridge himself has told us that such was the case.[‡]

---

[*] The members were: 1. Gunning Bedford, Member of Continental Congress and of the Constitutional Convention of 1787. 2. John Black. 3. H. H. Brackenridge, Judge of the Supreme Court of Pennsylvania and eminent in literature. 4. Donald Campbell. 5. Philip Freneau. 6. Charles McKnight, the most distinguished surgeon of his day. 7. James Madison, President of the United States. 8. Samuel Spring, a celebrated divine.

[†] MacLean's History of College of New Jersey, vol. i, p. 313.

[‡] Southern Literary Messenger, vol. viii, p. 2; also Hildeburn's Issue of the Press of Pennsylvania, vol. ii, p. 148.

The poem was to have been a joint production, but Brack-enridge, recognizing the slowness and heaviness of his own lines when compared with the graceful and sponta-neous verses of Freneau, wrote but a very small part, be-ing content to deliver it from the platform and to leave the honors of authorship to his friend.

In this commencement ode, "The Rising Glory of America," Freneau strikes the key-note of his life—resist-ance to Great Britain. The Massacre at Boston, March 5, 1770, is thus glanced at:

> Nor shall these angry tumults here subside,
> Nor murders cease through all these provinces,
> Till *foreign crowns have vanished from our view*
> And dazzle here no more—no more presume
> To own the spirit of fair liberty.
> Vengeance shall cut the thread, and Britain sure
> Will curse her fatal obstinacy.

The following is a clever bit of prophecy for a boy of nineteen; we find in it a constant and favorite theme of the poet—the greatness of America:

> I see, I see
> Freedom's established reign, cities and men,
> Numerous as sands upon the ocean shore,
> An Empire rising where the sun descends!
> The Ohio soon shall glide by many a town
> Of note; and where the Mississippi stream,
> By forests shaded, now runs sweeping on
> Nations shall grow, and States not less in fame
> Than Greece and Rome of old. We too shall boast
> Our Scipios, Solons, Catos, sages, chiefs
> That in the womb of time yet dormant lie,
> Waiting the joyous hour of life and light.

Freneau left college in September, 1771, with his mind full of epics and his heart full of liberty and hatred for oppression. He went to Philadelphia and pretended to read law, but probably he neglected his Blackstone for the society of wits, for he fell in with the whig leaders of the place and established a reputation as an exceedingly clever young scape-grace. It was while in Philadelphia in 1772

they proscribed me for four days and swore if I was caught in New York they would either Trounce or Maim me: but luckily I escaped with my goods to Princeton—where I remained till commencement—so much for this affair.

I have printed a poem in New York called the American Village, containing about 450 Lines, also a few short pieces added; I would send you one if I had a proper opportunity. The additional poems are—A Poem to the Nymph I Never Saw—The Miserable Life of a Pedagogue—and Stanzas on an ancient Dutch House on Long Island—As to the main poem it is damned by all good and judicious judges. My name is on the title page. This is called vanity by some—but "who so fond as youthful bards of fame?"

I arrived at this Somerset Academy the 18th of October and intend to remain here till next October. I am assistant to Mr. Brackenridge. This is the last time I shall enter into such a business; it worries me to death and by no means suits my "giddy, wandering brain."

I would go over for the gown this time two years, but the old hag Necessity has got such a prodigious grip of me that I fear I shall never be able to accomplish it. I believe if I cannot make this out I must turn quack, and indeed I am now reading Physic at my leisure hours, that is, when I am neither sleeping, hearing classes, or writing poetry—for these three take up all my time.

It is now late at night; not an hour ago I finished a little poem of about 400 lines, entitled a Journey to Maryland—being the sum of my adventures—it begins—

> From that famed town where Hudson's flood
> Unites with Streams perhaps as good;
> Muse has your bard begun to roam—

and I intend to write a terrible satire upon certain vicious persons of quality in New York—who have also used me ill—and print it next fall. It shall contain 5 or 600 lines. Sometimes I write pastorals to show my wit.

that he first saw himself in print. In that year the v
dictory ode came out in pamphlet form. The charm:
authorship seem to have allured him from serious st
for he soon abandoned law altogether. In the sprin
1772 he left Philadelphia and undertook to teach a sch
on Long Island but failed miserably. In the autumi
the same year we find him assisting his classmate Br
enridge in the management of an academy on the " E
ern Shore " of Maryland. The following letter to Ja
Madison, besides giving his experience as teacher, sh
how restless and aimless was his early manhood:

Somerset county in Maryland,

November 22, 177

Sir,

If I am not wrongly informed by my memory, I h
not seen you since last April, you may recollect I was t
undertaking a School at Flatbush on Long Island. I
tinued in it thirteen days—but—

> Long Island have I bid adieu,
> With all its brutish brainless crew.
> The youth of that detested place,
> Are void of reason and of grace,
> From Flatbush hills to Flatbush plains,
> Deep ignorance unrivalled reigns.

I am very poetical but excuse it. " *Si fama non v
ad aures,*" if you have not heard the rumor of this st
(which, by the by, is told in various taverns and eat
houses) you must allow me to be a little prolix with
Those who employed me were some gentlemen from N
York, some of them are bullies, some merchants, oth
scoundrels: They sent me eight children, the eldest
whom was 10 years old. Some could read, others s
and a few stammer over a chapter of the Bible—these w
my pupils and over these I was to preside. My sal
moreover was £40. There is something else relating
that I shall not at present mention. After I forsook th

Deep to the woods I sing a Shepherd's care,
Deep to the woods . . . call me there,
The last retreat of Love and Verse I go,
Verse made me mad at first—and will keep me so.

I should have been glad to have heard from you before now; while I was in college I had but a short participation of your agreeable friendship, and the few persons I converse with and yet fewer whose conversation I delight in, make me regret the loss of it. I have met a variety of rebuffs this year, which I forbear to mention. I look like an unmeaning Teague just turned out of the hold of an Irish Ship. Coming down hither I met with a rare adventure at Annapolis. I was destitute of even a brass farthing. I got clear very handsomely. Could one expect ever to see you again, if I travel through Virginia, I shall stop and talk with you a day or two. I should be very glad to receive a letter from you if it can be conveniently forwarded.

In short "*Non sum qualis eram*" as Partridge says in Tom Jones. My hair has grown like a mop, and I have a huge tuft of beard directly upon my chin. I want but five weeks of twenty-one years of age and already feel stiff with age. We have about 30 students in this academy who prey upon me like Leeches.

"When shall I quit this whimpering pack,
And hide my head in Accomack?"
Shall I leave them and go
Where Pokomokes long stream meandering flows—

Excuse this prodigious scrawl without style or sense. I send this by Mr. Luther Martin who will forward it to Col. Lee—and he to you I hope. Mr. Martin lives in Accomack in Virginia this side the bay.

Farewell and be persuaded I remain your truly humble servant and friend,

PH. F-R-E-N-E-A-U-[10]

---

[9] Illegible.
[10] Manuscript in the Archives of the Department of State at Washington.

This letter keeps us informed of Freneau's doings as far as the autumn of 1773, after which time we lose sight of him for a year or two. It is impossible to say where he was or what he was doing immediately after leaving Maryland, although we may confidently assume that on all occasions and in all places he did pretty much as he pleased. When we next meet with him he is in New York, the hot-bed of toryism, lampooning the tories. In 1775 we find him paying his respects in the columns of Hugh Gaine's " " Mercury " to General Gage, who had proclaimed in June of that year that the provinces were in a state of rebellion and out of the King's protection. Freneau professed, as rebels are wont to profess, to be deeply injured by the epithet " rebel."

> " *Rebels* you are "—the British Champion cries;
> *Truth,* stand thou forth and tell the wretch he *lies.*
> Rebels! and see this mock imperial lord
> Already threats these rebels with a *Cord!*
>
> *Americans!* at Freedom's fane adore!
> But trust to Britain and her flag no more.
> The generous genius of their isle has fled
> And left a mere impostor in his stead.
>
> To Arms! To Arms! and let the Murdering Sword
> Decide who best deserves the *hang-man's* cord.
> Nor think the hills of Canada too bleak
> When desperate freedom is the prize you seek.
> For *that* the call of honor bids you go
> O'er frozen lakes and mountains wrapped in snow.
>
> Haste! to your tents, in iron fetters bring
> Those slaves that serve a tyrant and a king.
> So just, so virtuous is your cause, I say
> Hell must prevail if Britain gains the day."

" Hugh Gaine, an Irishman, was the editor of the New York Mercury. His journal was edited in the interest of the whig party until the British troops approached New York in 1776. Then he went over to the royal cause. His double course is severely criticised by Freneau in his poem entitled: " The Political Biography of Hugh Gaine."

" The poem from which those lines are taken is addressed " To The Americans, on the rumored approach of the Hessian forces."

Thus the young man, without the slightest hesitation, and without any authority or responsibility, declares in the most fervid language for American Independence and proclaims a war upon England a twelve-month before Jefferson drew up the famous Declaration of the Fourth of July, 1776. In truth, such daring lines as these quickened the minds of the colonists and did much to create the sentiment which made the Declaration of Independence a plausible thing. To strong and brave minds, to the Henrys, and Otises and Hancocks, the only solution of the difficulties with the mother country was to be found in the absolute severance of all political ties. In this opinion Freneau shared to the fullest extent. In the year 1775 the opinion-makers of the Revolution were exceedingly busy and none were more active than the young poet. In verse, sometimes good, more frequently bad, always bold and always effective, he held up for the detestation of mankind, General Gage, Lord North, King George the Third, and the royal Governors, wherever he could find them. One of the shortest of these poems will serve to show how the cutting and slashing of the pen preceded the cutting and slashing of the sword, and how telling was Freneau's work as a precursor of a great movement. The poem is given entire.

EMANCIPATION FROM BRITISH DEPENDENCE.

Libera nos, Domine, Deliver us, O Lord,
Not only from British Dependence but also—

From a junto that labor for absolute power,
Where schemes disappointed have made them look sour,
From the lords of the council who fought against freedom
Who still follow on where delusion shall lead them,

From a group at St. James that slight our petitions,
And fools that are waiting for further submissions,
From a nation whose manners are rough and abrupt,
From scoundrels and rascals whom gold can corrupt,

34

From pirates sent out by command of the king
To murder and plunder but never to swing,
From Wallace and Graves and *Vipers* and *Roses* [13]
Whom, if Heaven pleases we will give bloody noses,

From the valliant Dunmore with his crew of banditti,
Who plunder Virginians at Williamsburg city,
From hot-headed Montague mighty to swear,
The little fat man, with his pretty white hair,

From bishops in Britain, who butchers are grown,
From slaves that would die for a smile of the throne,
From assemblies that vote against Congress proceedings,
(Who have seen the fruit of their stupid misleadings),

From Tyron, [14] the mighty, who flies from our city,
And swelled with importance disdains the committee;
(But since he is pleased to proclaim us his foes,
What the devil care we where the devil he goes);

From the caitiff Lord North, who would bind us in chains,
From our noble King Log, with his tooth-full of brains,
Who dreams and is certain (when taking a nap)
He has conquered our lands, as they lay on his map,

From a Kingdom that bullies and hectors and swears,
I send up to heaven my wishes and prayers,
That we disunited, may freemen be still,
And Britain go on—to be damn'd if she will.

The young verse-maker was sure as to the course to be pursued by America, but he was not sure as to the problem that confronted his individual life. The poetry in his nerves unbalanced him and weakened his purposes. His property in New Jersey was neglected, and gradually began to slip from his hands. The young patriot followed his instinct—often a surer guide than reason—and abandoned himself to verse-making. The muse he chose was satire. The troublous times, he said, admitted of no other choice.

In doing this Freneau was building better than he knew. The pieces which he sent to the press every week were

---

[13] " Wallace and Graves," British naval officers. " Vipers " and " Roses," the names of two ships in the English service.
[14] The last royal governor of New York.

rarely ineffectual. They made the tories wince and they inspired the whigs with hope and courage. They brought him no money, yet they did better than this. They rendered the country an important service, and they brought their author lasting fame: they made him the " Poet of the Revolution."

CHAPTER II

THE POET OF THE REVOLUTION

In 1776, Freneau left New York and its tory citizens to
their own devices and embarked upon a vessel bound for
the Danish West Indies. According to one account he
sailed as the agent of a New York trading firm; another
account states that he shipped as a common sailor and
worked his way up to the post of captain.[1] It is certain
that he learned the art of navigation and that he soon became the master of a ship. From this time on we shall
find him a rover, now upon the sea, now upon the land;
now a captain, now an editor, but always a poet, writing
for the American cause.

His first voyage was to the Virgin Islands, where he
seems to have remained for some time. He fell in love
with the natural beauties of the southern isles, and con-
ceived a disgust for their institutions. Slavery was always
an abomination in his eyes. The mild form of northern
servitude was distasteful to him, but the degraded condition of the West Indian slave awakened the warmest indig-
nation in his generous mind. In a poem descriptive of the
island of Santa Cruz, he expresses in sorrowful strain his
repugnance to the ugly form of human bondage found
there. "It casts," he says in a preface to this poem, "a
shade over the native charms of the country; it blots out
the beauty of the eternal spring which Providence has
there ordained to reign; and amidst all the profusions of
beauties which nature has scattered—the brightness of the
heavens, the mildness of the air, and the luxuriance of the
vegetable kingdom—it leaves me melancholy and discon-

---

[1] American Magazine of History, vol. xvii, p. 124.

solate. Thus the earth which, were it not for the lust of
pride and dominion, might be an earthly paradise, is, by
the ambition and overbearing nature of mankind, rendered
an eternal scene of desolation, woe, and horror: the weak
go to the wall while the strong prevail." [1]

This hatred of slavery was not an evanescent passion of
youth doomed through the hardening processes of years
to die; it was a settled principle of his life and conduct.
In another poem, written in middle life, he thus holds up
the torch of liberty, and with it runs ahead of his times by
half a century:

> " O come the time and haste the day
> When man shall man no longer crush;
> When reason shall enforce her sway,
> Nor these fair regions raise one blush,
> Where still the *African* complains,
> And mourns his yet unbroken chains." [2]

" In after life," says Duyckinck, " when the poet himself
became the owner of slaves in New Jersey, he uniformly
treated them with kindness, manumitted them in advance
of the Emancipation Act in the State, and supported on
the farm those of them who were too old to take care of
themselves."

When Freneau returned to America, independence had
been declared and the Revolution was progressing with
varying fortune. The poet threw himself into the struggle with a poet's ardor. One of his first acts after fairly
getting upon land was to ratify the Declaration of Independence in four hundred spirited verses. This poem, entitled " American Independent," was printed at Philadelphia
in 1778 at the press of Robert Bell, the printer of Thomas
Paine's " Common Sense." When foreign troops were
ravaging the land, when the principal cities were in possession of the enemy, when the Continental Army at Val-
ley Forge was starving, when toryism threatened to wreck
the cause of liberty, Freneau's animating voice was heard.

[1] United States Magazine, 1779.   [2] Poems, edition of 1795.

Americans! revenge your country's wrongs
To you the honor of the deed belongs.
Expel yon thieves from these polluted lands,
Expect no peace [4] till haughty Britain yields,
Till humbled Britons quit your ravaged fields.
No dull debates or tedious councils know,
But rush at once embodied on your foe!
Your injured country groans while yet they stay,
Attend her groans, and force their hosts away.
Your mighty wrongs the tragic muse shall trace,
Your gallant deeds shall fire a future race.
To you may Kings and potentates appeal,
You may the doom of jarring nations seal.
A glorious empire rises bright and new,
Firm be its base, and it must rest on you.
Fame o'er the mighty pile extends her wings,
Remote from princes, bishops, lords, and kings,—
Those fancied gods, who famed through every shore,
Mankind have fashioned and like fools adore.

Freneau kept his eye upon the events of the day and cheered and exhorted and celebrated as the poet-general of a revolution should. But he was not content to lurk and write. In 1778 New Jersey became the battle-ground of the revolution, and the region of the poet's home was filled with the soldiery of the contending parties. The battle of Monmouth was fought almost within sight of his ancestral door. Philip shouldered his gun for the defense of his fireside. He entered the army as a private and was promoted to the rank of sergeant.[5] His career as a soldier was brief and unimportant, but it served to show the stuff of which he was made.

Freneau soon laid down the sword for the pen. The year following the battle of Monmouth (1779) was a busy one, and was more profitably spent than if he had remained in the field. Poem after poem came out to revive the flagging spirits of the revolutionists. His old college-mate and colleague in poetry, Hugh Brackenridge, was in Philadelphia trying to drive the wolf from the door by

---

[4] Aimed at Lord North's "Conciliating Bills" which arrived in New York in April, 1778, and which conciliated nobody.
[5] Jerseymen in the Revolution, p. 465.

editing "The United States Magazine, A Repository of History, Politics and Literature." The columns of this periodical were open to Freneau and he became one of its principal contributors. Brackenridge used a free lance and his magazine was feared and hated.⁶ In addition to the poems that were written on the voyage to the West Indies, there appeared in this magazine Freneau's "King George the Third's Soliloquy," and his "Dialogue between his Britannic Majesty and Mr. Fox." The object of these pieces was to urge on to carnage and conquest rather than to awaken feelings of the sublime and beautiful. They are blunt, coarse appeals to the Americans to "up and at the bloody red coats," and there is no poetry in them. The British army is characterized as a band of devils that it would be a mercy to rid the earth of. George III in soliloquy, thus describes his method of raising a force to march against America:

> Is there a robber close in Newgate hemmed?
> Is there a cut-throat fettered and condemned?
> Haste loyal slaves, to George's standard come,
> Attend his lectures when you hear the drum!
> Your chain I break; for better days prepare;
> Come out my friends from prison and from care.
> Far to the West I plan your desperate sway,—
> There 'tis no sin to ravage, burn, and slay,
> There without fear your bloody aims pursue,
> And show mankind what English thieves can do.

In the dialogue between Fox and King George, the liberal-minded and far-seeing statesman thus advised his monarch:

> In one short sentence take my whole advice,
> (It is no time to flatter and be nice)
> With all your soul for instant peace contend,
> Then shall you be your country's truest friend;
> Peace, instant peace, may stay your tottering throne,
> But wars and death and blood can profit none.
> Withdraw your arms from the American shore,
> And vex her ocean with your fleet no more;
> Implore the friendship of the injured states,
> Nor longer strive against the stubborn fates.

---

⁶ Southern Literary Messenger, vol. vii, p. 3.

But the haughty monarch would not listen to Fox, or to any one else. The war went on by land and by sea, and whether by land or by sea, Freneau was prompt to record in "superior [?] lays" the glorious deeds of the Americans. In 1779, the gallant Paul Jones of the *Bon Homme Richard*, gloriously defeated Captain Pearson of the *Serapis*, and the victory was duly celebrated by our poet, and the victor thus urged on to further conquest:

> Go on great man to scourge the foe,
> And bid these haughty Britons know
> They to our thirteen states shall bend;
> The stars that veiled in dark attire
> Long glimmered with a feeble fire,
> But radiant now ascend.
>
> Bend to the stars that flaming rise
> On western worlds, more brilliant skies,
> Fair Freedom's reign restored.
> So when the Magi came from far
> Beheld the God-attending star,
> They trembled and adored.

"The United States Magazine" died in the first year of its life and its talented editor abandoned journalism and sought and gained distinction in law. Freneau was in no sense the editor of this magazine, as has been stated so frequently. He simply gave a helping hand to his friend Brackenridge, who was the real proprietor.

After the magazine had gone under, Freneau ventured again upon the sea. This time he sailed for the West Indies with letters of marque against British commerce, commanding the *Aurora*, a smart little craft fitted out for privateering.¹ But Freneau's naval achievements were destined to be of no greater importance than his career as a land soldier. When his vessel was well beyond the

---

¹ See Griswold's Male Poets of America, p. 32, and Alibone's Dictionary of Authors.

² Forman's Journey down the Ohio, p. 10. From Freneau's own account of this voyage, it does not appear that he was the actual commander. See his "Some Account of the Capture of the ship *Aurora*" recently published for the first time.

capes at the mouth of the Delaware Bay, she was pursued, and after a sharp engagement, was captured by the British cruiser *Iris.* The captives were taken to New York and confined in a British prison-ship that lay moored off the battery. Freneau was placed upon the *Scorpion,* where he was kept two months, and then, when dangerously sick of a fever, was removed to the hospital-ship *Hunter,* "to all hospitals disgrace." From the *Hunter* in a short time he escaped, broken and emaciated by the cruel experiences through which he had passed. Of course the incident became the occasion of a poem. The whole story is told in "The British Prison-Ship," in four cantos, written and published in 1781.

Freneau wrote nothing for the American cause that was more effective than this piece. In it the cruelty and inhumanity of the British were depicted by the hand of one who had himself seen and suffered. "The picturesque incidents of the voyage which is described; the animated action of the capture; the melancholy circumstances of the prison-ship contrasted with the happy scenes of the shore; the stern terrors of the Hospital, are all in Freneau's best vein." [*] The following lines are too realistic to be untrue:

> Such food they sent to make complete our woes,—
> It looked like carrion torn from hungry crows:
> Such vermin vile on every joint were seen,
> So black, corrupted, mortified, and lean,
> That once we tried to move our flinty chief,
> And thus addressed him, holding up the beef:
> " See, Captain, see! what rotten bones we pick;
> What kills the healthy cannot cure the sick;
> Not dogs on such by Christian men are fed,
> And see, good master, see what lousy bread! "
> " Your meat or bread," this man of death replied,
> " 'Tis not my care to manage or provide—
> But this, base rebel dogs, I'd have you know
> That better than your merit we bestow."

When the poet escaped from the clutches of the British, he returned to Philadelphia and slowly regained his health.

---

[*] Poems of the Revolution, edited by E. A. Duyckinck, p. 10.

He soon resumed his post as verse-chronicler of the revolution and followed with anxious eyes the closing scenes
of the struggle. On the eighth of October, 1781, he addressed these savage and semi-prophetic lines to the proud
Cornwallis:

> Would thou at last with Washington engage,
> Sad object of his pity not his rage?
> See round thy posts how terribly advance
> The chiefs, the armies, and the fleets of France.
> Fight while you can for warlike Rochambeau
> Aims at your head his last decisive blow;
> Unnumbered ghosts from earth untimely sped,
> Can take no rest till you like them are dead.
> Then die, my lord; that only chance remains
> To wipe away dishonorable stains.
> For small advantage would your capture bring—
> The plundering servant of a bankrupt king.[10]

A month later came Yorktown and the consummation
of American Independence. Freneau, like all Americans,
hated Cornwallis bitterly, and gloated over the fallen
chief in coarse and careless verse. With this malediction
he sped him from our shores:

> Now curst with life, a foe to man and God,
> Like Cain we drive you to the land of Nod;
> He with a brother's blood his hands did stain,
> One brother he,—you have a thousand slain.
> And may destruction rush with speedy wing,
> Low as yourself to drag each tyrant king.[11]

The war was over but there was aftermath enough to
keep the patriotic pen of Freneau in motion. When the
traitor Arnold left New York in December, 1781, the
poet's fiercest and choicest curse went with him; the battle
of Eutaw Springs was celebrated in a lyric that Scott
learned by heart and regarded as one of the finest things
in the language; Washington, on his way to Virginia was
greeted in Philadelphia by a worthy ode; the rejoicing over
the recognition of National Independence stirred the poet

---

[10] *Poems Relating to the Revolution,* p. 121.   [11] *Ibid.,* p. 132.

to one of his highest flights." Taking it altogether, the
year 1782 was a most productive one. Freneau seems to
have settled down to literature with the purpose of making
a living out of it. He wrote constantly and much, both
in prose and verse, for " The Freeman's Journal," throughout the three years of its existence.

Freneau was now enjoying fame as poet, essayist and
patriot, but money was not forthcoming. America was
too poor to pay for literature and the poet was driven to
seek bread upon the water. Next to literature he loved
the sea. He became captain of a vessel and it was a common occurrence of his life to sail down to the West Indies
with a cargo of grain, and bring up a cargo of molasses
and poetry. In 1784, we find him wandering about among
the ruins of old Port Royal and riming the sad condition
of that unfortunate and desolate place. For five or six
years without interruption, he led the hardy life of a tar.

In April, 1789, George Washington proceeded in triumph through the States to New York to be inaugurated
as president. "Thursday last between two and three
o'clock," says the "Gazette of the United States" of
April 25, 1789, "the most illustrious president of the
United States arrived in this city. At Elizabethtown he
was received by a deputation of three senators and five
representatives of the United States, and the officers of the
state and corporation, with whom he embarked on the
barge for the purpose of wafting him across the bay. It is
impossible to do justice to an attempt to describe the
scene exhibited in his Excellency's approach to the city."
In another column in the same number of the Gazette is
this notice:

" Thursday, April 23, arrived here the schooner *Columbia, P. Freneau*, in 8 days from Charleston. On board
was Dr. King from S. America, with a collection of natural curiosities, particularly a male and female ourang-
outang."

⁑ Poems of the Revolution, pp. 201, 260, 270.

Captain Freneau, with Dr. King and his monkeys on
board, brought his ship into line and sailed up the bay with
the gay and magnificent procession of boats that escorted
the president-elect to the capital city. When the poet
landed he found himself in the midst of old friends. There
was his room-mate and classmate, James Madison, the
young "father of the constitution"; there was the ambitious and unscrupulous Aaron Burr; and, the rising Henry
B. Livingston, boon companions at Princeton. These
men, now powerful in the nation, were glad to grasp the
hand of their old friend, for they recognized in him one
almost as famous as themselves and one not inferior in
talent. Freneau was charmed by the new and invigorating
associations of New York life. He gave up his ship and
again took up his pen. He made friends with the leading
democrats, and was soon conspicuous as a champion of
democracy. The pen of a contemporary has left us a picture of him as he moves about in printing offices and
government halls, or stands chatting with senators and
generals. " He was somewhat below the ordinary height;
in person, he was thin yet muscular; his countenance was
traced by care; he was mild in enunciation, neither rapid
nor slow, but clear, distinct and emphatic. His forehead
was rather beyond the medium elevation; his eyes a dark
gray, occupying a socket deeper than common; his hair
a beautiful iron gray. He was free of all ambitious dis-
plays. His habitual expression was pensive. His dress
might have passed for that of a farmer." [13]

Freneau found employment as a writer for the New
York Daily Advertiser.[14] He does not seem to have been

---

[13] Sketch of Freneau in Dr. J. W. Francis' Cyclopedia of American Literature, vol. i, p. 333.

[14] " About 1790," says Major Samuel Forman in his " Journey
down the Ohio," " Captain Freneau married my sister Eleanor."
Eleanor Forman was the daughter of Samuel Forman of New
Jersey, one of Freneau's neighbors, and a hero of the revolution.
The poet and Eleanor seemed to have been drawn together by
an affinity of tastes, for she was a verse-maker as well as he.

its editor, as Hudson and others assert, but its manager or superintendent—a kind of man-of-all-work.[15] One of his co-laborers upon the Advertiser was John Pintard, a warm personal friend, and the translating-clerk in the Department of State. Freneau worked vigorously for the Advertiser, and he was soon recognized in political circles as a strong ally of the anti-federalists.

In 1790, Thomas Jefferson came to New York to assume the duties of Secretary of State. He had just come from Paris where he had been an eye witness of the storming of the Bastile and had learned from terrible object-lessons to respect the power of the masses. When he arrived in New York, his democracy was at a white heat and he eagerly set about building up a democratic party. He met Freneau and found him a congenial spirit. The true eye of the great politician saw in the poet good timber for the edifice it was his intention to rear. Jefferson, as a well-known patron of letters, was in a position to make overtures to any man of distinguished talents. An opportunity to render Freneau good service soon presented itself. When the government removed to Philadelphia early in 1791, John Pintard, the French translator in Jefferson's office, resigned his place, declining to leave New York for the pitiable stipend of two hundred and fifty dollars per annum, the amount appropriated for the translating-clerk. Madison and Henry Lee urged Jefferson to appoint Freneau to the position made vacant by Pintard. Jefferson gladly acceded to their request, and on February 28, 1791, wrote to Freneau as follows:

"Sir: The clerkship for foreign languages in my office is vacant. The salary indeed, is very low, being but two

---

The writer has seen in manuscript some very clever verses written by Mrs. Freneau. For several years before marriage, their correspondence is said to have been conducted largely in rhyme. The Freneau home, when we get glimpses of it, was a happy one, albeit unthrifty.

[15] Hudson's Journalism in America, p. 175.

hundred and fifty dollars; but also, it gives so little to do as not to interfere with any other calling the person may choose which would not absent him from the seat of government. I was told a few days ago that it might perhaps be convenient for you to accept it. If so, it is at your service. It requires no other qualification than a moderate knowledge of the French. Should any thing better turn up within my department that might suit you, I should be very happy to bestow it as well. Should you conclude to accept the present, you may consider it as engaged to you, only be so good as to drop me a line informing me of your resolution." [28]

We have not Freneau's reply to this letter but we know that he was in no hurry to accept the offer. It was his intention to remove from New York, his work upon the Advertiser rendering him but slender returns; but he had misgivings about going to Philadelphia. His immediate project was to settle in New Jersey and to establish a country newspaper, a plan which he long cherished and one which he finally carried out. Madison, however, saw the value of the man as a democratic publicist and would not listen to his burying himself in the obscurity of a New Jersey village. He went to Freneau and reasoned with him, endeavoring to make him sensible of the advantages that Philadelphia offered for his private undertaking over a small country town. He explained the nature of the services required of him as translator in the Department of State. Freneau had thought that he would be expected to turn English into French, and feeling his incompetency for this work, delicacy forbade him to accept the position. Madison dissipated this objection by assuring him that no such task would be required of him. Freneau listened to the solicitations of his friend and decided to go to Philadelphia at once. Madison wrote to Jefferson stating that he might expect Freneau in Philadelphia in a very short

---

[28] Jefferson's Works, vol. iii, p. 215.

time. The letter contains a tribute to Freneau's character and genius, and principles, and closes with these words: "It is certain that there is not to be found in the whole catalogue of American Printers [Editors] a single name that can approach rivalship.""

But Freneau halted in New Jersey, and Jefferson concluded that he had abandoned the notion of going to Philadelphia. On May 9 Jefferson wrote to Madison: "Your favor of the first came to hand on the third. Mr. Freneau has not followed it. I suppose, therefore, he has changed his mind back again, for which I am sorry." "
A few days after this Jefferson wrote to Thomas Mann Randolph, his son-in-law, as follows:

"I enclose you Bache's as well as Fenno's papers. You will have perceived that the latter is a paper of pure toryism, disseminating the doctrine of monarchy, aristocracy, and the exclusion of the people. We have been trying to get another weekly or half-weekly set up, excluding advertisements, so that it might go through the States and furnish a whig vehicle of intelligence. We hoped at one time to have persuaded Freneau to set up here but failed." "

Jefferson did not intend to lose Freneau if he could help it. Further pressure was brought to bear upon the editor. Gen. Henry Lee, another friend, wrote to him and urged him to embrace the opportunities of a career at the seat of government." The general promised aid in securing subscribers for the projected paper and, (Parton says) advanced money for the enterprise." Jefferson, on July 21, 1791, again wrote to Madison with the view of getting Freneau. "I am sincerely sorry," he says, "that Freneau has declined coming here. Though the printing business be

" Writings of Madison, vol. i, p. 535.
" Jefferson's Writings, vol. v, p. 330.
" Ibid., vol. v, p. 336.
" Randall's Life of Jefferson, vol. ii, p. 74.
" Parton's Life of Jefferson, p. 433.

sufficiently full here, yet I think he would set out on such advantageous grounds as to have been sure of success. His own genius, in the first place, is so superior to that of his competitors. I should have given him the perusal of all my letters of foreign intelligence and all foreign newspapers, the publication of all proclamations and other public notices within my department, and the printing of the laws, which added to his salary would have been a considerable aid. Besides this, Fenno's being the only weekly paper and under general condemnation for its toryism and its incessant efforts to over-turn the government, Freneau would have found that ground as good as unoccupied."

This encouragement from such influential quarters finally caused Freneau to abandon his original scheme and settle in Philadelphia. On the twenty-fifth of July, four days after Jefferson's last letter to Madison, he himself wrote to Madison:

"Some business detains me here [in New Jersey] a day or two longer from returning to New York. When I come, which I expect will be upon Thursday, if you shall not have left the city, I will give you a decisive answer relative to printing my paper at the seat of government instead of New York. If I can get Mr. Childs to be connected with me on a tolerable plan I believe I shall sacrifice other considerations and transfer myself to Philadelphia."

Freneau came to terms with the printer, Childs, and in a short time repaired to Philadelphia, leaving his family temporarily behind him. In the course of a few days after his arrival he received the following document:

"Philip Freneau is hereby appointed clerk for foreign languages in the office of Secretary of State, with a salary of two hundred and fifty dollars a year, to commence from the time he shall take the requisite oaths of qualification. Given under my hand and seal this 16th day of August, 1791,   THOMAS JEFFERSON." [21]

---

[21] Jefferson MS. Archives of State Department at Washington.

This is the story of Freneau's coming to Philadelphia to set up a paper and of his appointment to an office under Jefferson. It is a simple story and one that is not suggestive of crookedness upon the part of any of the persons connected with it. As far as Freneau is concerned, his course was one of absolute single-mindedness throughout. He intended to start a newspaper of his own, and a democratic newspaper at that. If he did not set up one in New Jersey, then he would start one in New York. Jefferson, Madison, and other democrats, hearing of this, held out, in a perfectly honorable way, inducements for him to establish his paper in Philadelphia, and after due reflection he adopted the counsel of his friends. Those friends knew that he intended to edit a paper—that indeed he must do something of the kind or starve. They knew, moreover, that he was a fierce and uncompromising democrat and that he would conduct the paper according to his own notions. What their motives were in getting such a man to come to the seat of government is very easy to determine. They wanted the influence of his pen for party purposes. Whether Jefferson was justified in using patronage for the accomplishment of his purpose is a problem of ethics for those who are interested in the question to solve. It may be here remarked that from the beginning of our government to the present day influential editors have fared very well in the matter of federal appointments. With Freneau, the establishing of his paper in Philadelphia was purely a matter of business, and it is difficult to conceive how there could have arisen in his mind any quibbling as to the rightfulness or wrongfulness of his earning a little additional money by translating. The matter would not be worth referring to, if, as we shall see later, so much had not been made of it by the enemies of Freneau and of Jefferson.

We shall now take up a chapter in Freneau's history which has not received the consideration it deserves. We shall follow Freneau in his career as an editor. We all know something of him in a vague sort of way as a poet. We know a little of him, too, as an editor, but, unfortunately what we know of him as an editor is false knowledge. Washington Irving called him a "barking cur," and succeeding historians down to Goldwin Smith, who refers to him as a "reptile journalist," have been content to perpetuate a false and unjust estimate of the man.

CHAPTER III

THE DEMOCRATIC EDITOR

The plan and purposes of the new paper were published at considerable length. The Gazette was to appear every Wednesday and Saturday;[1] the subscription price was to be three dollars *per annum;* the news published was to be of national character, especial attention being promised to the doings of the national government; the columns of the Gazette were to be open to all original and interesting productions whether prose or verse; political discussion was to be conducted with perfect fairness and the greatest latitude; the debates of congress and reports of departments were to be printed; all important books were to be reviewed; advertisements were to be allotted a certain space and were not to encroach upon the columns intended for general reading matter.

The title of the paper, "The National Gazette," suggests the aims of its founder. It was to be a paper for circulation in all parts of the union. It was to be an organ with national influence and a national constituency as opposed to those papers which appealed to local constituencies and which rarely found their way out of the neighborhood in which they were printed. This was the idea of the editor and his advisers, and every effort was made to keep the paper cosmopolitan and to get it into distant parts.

Freneau pushed forward the publication of the Gazette and the first number came from the press several days before it was announced to appear. In the first issues there was nothing to shadow forth that violent partisanship which later was to make its editor one of the best hated

[1] It was actually published every Monday and Thursday.

men in America. In one respect, indeed, it offended from the beginning the opinion of a large and influential element of the American people. It supported without reserve the principles of the French revolution. Its columns were filled with equality and fraternity, and Tom Paine and Rousseau. Aside from this undisguised endorsement of what was then to many minds, political heresy, its tone was mild, and its articles harmless and colorless. Its professed policy was broad and patriotic. It early maintained the doctrine that the union between the states should be social and commercial as well as political. " The interests of the northern and southern states are inseparable forever. It seems to have been the design of nature in her formation and distribution of that part of North America known by the name of the United States, that a mutual dependence should take place between the northern and southern inhabitants."[2] But the tendency of the paper was unmistakable. It appealed to the common people as the true rulers of government. Its evident purpose was to evoke and energize the spirit of democracy.

Was there need for such a paper? Was the spirit of democracy flagging and the tide running toward a government, strong, centralized, and aristocratic? Was the constitution, as Jefferson says it was, galloping toward monarchy? We cannot understand Freneau and the part he played in public affairs until we have found answers to these questions, and to answer them we must try to get as clear a notion as possible of the state of political opinion in the United States in 1791.

To do this let us begin with the rulers. Let us interrogate those who were in the saddle at the time, and determine the direction they were galloping by the tendency of their thought; for as men think, so are they.

If we begin with the President, there can be no doubt of Washington's perfect loyalty to the constitution and to

---

[2] National Gazette, November, 1791.

a republican form of government. In 1786, indeed, he recognized that times were changing, and that monarchy was in the air,[3] but he deprecated with the utmost horror the progress of monarchical sentiment. Freneau has attested to the soundness of the great chief's republicanism in these lines:

> "Oh Washington, thrice glorious name!
> What due rewards can man decree?
> *Empires* are far below thy aim,
> And *sceptres* have no charm for thee.
> *Virtue* alone has your regard,
> And she must be your great reward."

We pass from the President to the Vice-president. John Adams has written many hundreds of pages upon the subject of government, but human reason cannot fathom his meaning and what he really thought will never be known. Madison, open and above board, spoke of him to Washington as aiming at mixed monarchy,[5] but Adams said he was not aiming at monarchy, and we must believe he knew his motives better than Madison knew them. We cannot get from his writings what Adams thought, but we can learn from them what he *felt*. He hated democracy, he loved a strong government. "Democracy,"[6] he says, "never has been and never can be so desirable as aristocracy or monarchy, but while it lasts, is more bloody than either. Remember, democracy never lasts long. It soon wastes,

---

[3] Sparks' Life and Writings of Washington, vol. ix, p. 187.

[4] An English reviewer of the day thought he understood Adams: "The great and leading idea which runs through the ingenious and learned works of Mr. Adams is that a mixture of the three powers, the regal, the aristocratical and the democratical, properly balanced, comprises the most perfect form of government." American Daily Advertiser, Nov., 1792. Such an interpretation must have been based upon such statements as these: "The English Constitution is the only scientific government." John Adams' Works, vol. vi, p. 118. "A hereditary first magistrate would perhaps be preferable to an elective one."

[5] In a conversation with the President in 1792, Writings of Madison, vol. i, p. 558.

[6] John Adams' Works, vol. vi, p. 483.

exhausts, and murders itself. There never was a democracy that did not commit suicide." And again: "It is true and I rejoice in it, that our president has more power than the stadt-holders, the doges, the archons, or the kings of Lacedaemon." He expresses his profound distrust of self-government in these words: "The proposition that the people are the best keepers of their own liberties is not true. They are the worst conceivable, they are no keepers at all; they can neither judge, act, think, or will, as a political body. Individuals have conquered themselves; nations and large bodies never."[1] In a letter to his democratic cousin, Samuel Adams, John Adams, in a few inadvertent words, betrays his feelings towards popular liberty. Samuel Adams had advanced the proposition that the love of liberty is interwoven in the soul of man. John Adams, candidate for popular favor, replied: "So it is, according to La Fontaine, in that of a wolf."[2] Late in life, John Adams said that his political downfall was largely due to the writings of Philip Freneau.[3] He would more justly have attributed his retirement to his own writings.

When we come to Washington's first cabinet we find a house divided against itself. Relying upon his own vast authority and the rectitude of his intentions, the president invited to assist him in governing, two men whose views upon government diverged as widely as possible. Thomas Jefferson and Alexander Hamilton, by every principle and implication of their being, were unfitted to work together, and Washington's attempt at a mixed cabinet failed. In a short time the imperious and imperial Hamilton dominated Washington and the administration, and Jefferson was forced to retire.

What were Hamilton's views upon government? If he could have had his will, what form of government would

---

[1] Works of John Adams, vol. i, p. 587.
[2] Works of Samuel Adams.   [3] Works of John Adams.

have been instituted? What was the tendency of our government when it was under his direction? To get an answer to this question, we may take the testimony first of a friend, then of an enemy. Gouverneur Morris, an intimate friend and co-worker in politics, said of Hamilton: " He hated republican government because he confounded it with democratic government. One marked trait of the general's character was his pertinacious adherence to opinions once formed. He never failed on every occasion to advocate the excellence of and avow his attachment to monarchical government."[10] Thomas Jefferson corroborates this language by putting the following words in Hamilton's mouth; words, Jefferson avers, which were written down almost immediately after they were spoken: " I own it is my opinion, although I do not publish it in Dan and Beersheba, that the present government is not that which will answer the ends of society by giving stability and protection to its rights, and that it will probably be expedient to go to the British form."[11]

Hamilton's correspondence is replete with lugubrious apprehensions that the government by the people might fail.[12] The people were to him " *informe ingens, cui lumen ademptum.*"[18] In a letter to Theodore Sedgwick he speaks of democracy as a virulent poison, that was threatening to destroy the life of the nation.[14] In 1802, when he had been unhorsed and Jefferson was in the saddle, he writes to his old friend and fellow-aristocrat, Morris, bitterly complaining of his fate: " Mine is an odd destiny. I am still laboring to *prop the frail and worthless fabric.* Yet I have the murmurs of its friends no less than the curses of its foes for my reward. What can I do better than withdraw from the scene? Every day proves to me more and more

[10] Sparks' Gouverneur Morris, Life and Works, vol. iii, p. 260.
[11] Ford's " Jefferson's Writings," vol. i, p. 169.
[12] See Hamilton's Works, vol. v, p. 441; vol. vi, p. 54; vol. iii, p. 260.
[13] Ibid., vol. vi, p. 540.   [14] Ibid., vol. vi, p. 568.

that this American world was not made for me." [13] At a banquet in New York, in reply to a toast Hamilton uttered these remarkable words: " Your people, sir, your people are a great beast." [14] But enough of quotations. Everybody knows now as well as Jefferson knew in 1791 that Alexander Hamilton hated democracy and that he had little faith in the government that he had helped to establish.

It is of interest to note also what the lesser lights, what senators and representatives and diplomats of the time thought of democracy. The young and eloquent Fisher Ames, the confidential friend of Hamilton and a leader in the house of representatives, declared democracy to be the isthmus of a middle state, nothing in itself. Like death it was the dismal passport to a more dismal hereafter. He thought our nation began self-government without education for it. " Like negroes," he says, " freed after grown up to man's estate, we are incapable of learning and practicing the great art of taking care of ourselves." [15] He greets Hamilton's sympathetic ears with these words: " Our government is becoming a mere democracy which has never been tolerable or long tolerated." [16] And again, in an explosion of disgust and despair he cries: " Our country is too big for union, too sordid for patriotism, too democratic for liberty! What is to become of it, He who made it best knows." [17]

Gouverneur Morris has answered for Hamilton and may now answer for himself on the subject of democratic government. Writing from Paris to Rufus King he says: " The people, or rather the populace—a thing which, thank God, is unknown in America—are flattered with the idea that they are under no restraint except such as might be

---

[13] Hamilton's Works, vol. vi, p. 530.
[14] Adams' History of the United States, vol. i, p. 85.
[15] Works of Fisher Ames, vol. i, p. 224.
[16] Hamilton's Works, vol. vi, p. 201.
[17] Ames' Works, vol. i, p. 327.

inspired by magistrates of their own choice." [20] This haughty lieutenant of Hamilton's having narrowly escaped the fury of that same Parisian populace, wished to check the power of the people in his own country by a strong government. He believed that a national law should repeal any state law, and was for a senate for life, appointed by the chief magistrate. The body should consist of men of wealth and of aristocratic spirit—one that would "lord it through pride."

Theodore Sedgwick, speaker of the House of Representatives, had no faith in the manner of electing the president. [21] John Jay, Chief Justice of the Supreme Court, doubted whether the people could long govern themselves in an "equal, uniform and orderly manner." [22] Oliver Wolcott, Comptroller of the Treasury, and successor of Hamilton as Secretary, believed that our system of government would fail. [23] Chauncey Goodrich, a leader in politics wrote: "Our greatest danger is from the antagonism of levelism. What folly is it that has set the world agog to be all equal to French barbers?" George Cabot, senator from Massachusetts, held the belief that "Democracy in its natural operation is the government of the worst." [24]

Such was the faith, or rather lack of faith, of our federal fathers. Such were the avowed opinions regarding self-government held by those who were administering the government, making its laws, conducting its diplomacy, pronouncing its justice, at the period when Freneau set up his National Gazette in Philadelphia. Washington warned the federal leaders against their monarchical notions, reminding them that it was but a step from thinking to speaking and but another to acting. [25] And they did

[20] Life of Rufus King, vol. i, p. 432.
[21] Hamilton's Works, vol. vi, p. 517.
[22] Gill's "Administration of Washington and Adams," vol. i, p. 390.
[23] Ibid., p. 88.   [24] Lodge's Cabot, p. 341.
[25] Sparks' "Life and Writings of Washington," vol. ix, p. 187.

act as far as prudence would permit. Hamilton tried to hedge Washington around " with a divinity that did befit a King." Titles and royal trappings were employed to dazzle and awe; measures were introduced into congress under Hamilton's doctrine of " implied powers " that made democrats like Maclay and Madison stand aghast. Hamilton and Hamiltonism ruled not only in the cabinet but in the legislature also. It was charged that the Treasurer in British fashion cracked his whip over congress,[26] and " converted the legislature into a committee of sanction," and Washington himself was accused of " treading on the neck of the senate." [27]

The organ upon which the federalists relied to make public opinion for their cause was John Fenno's " Gazette of the United States." This paper was started in New York but was moved to Philadelphia when the government was transferred to that place." Fenno was completely under Hamilton's control and the columns of his Gazette were filled with the monarchical notions of his patron. The following extract, taken from the writings of " Tablet " who contributed, every week, something upon the subject of government, will give an idea of the spirit of Fenno's paper:

" *Take away thrones and crowns from among men and there will soon be an end of all dominion and justice.* There must be some adventitious properties infused into the government to give it energy and spirit, or the selfish, turbulent passions of men can never be controlled. This has occasioned that artificial splendor and dignity that are to be found in the courts of many nations. The people of the United States may probably be induced to regard

---

[26] Mercer in a speech in congress said: " I have long remarked in this house that the executive, or rather the treasury department, was really the efficient legislature of the country. The House of Representatives is converted into a committee of sanction."

[27] Maclay's Journal, p. 131.

[28] Hudson's Journalism in America, p. 18.

and obey the laws without requiring the experiment of courts and titled monarchs. In proportion as we become populous and wealthy must the tone of the government be strengthened." *

Americans were invited to distrust their fitness for sovereignty, "for the experience of past ages proved that whenever the people have exercised in themselves the three powers, the democracy is immediately changed into anarchy. Violent orators agitate the multitude as the winds toss the waves, and the people agitated by demagogues have committed all excesses." Titles were upheld as the essential features of a vigorous government. The argument for them was simple and cogent. There are differences in men, in talent, in wealth, in position; therefore, there should be titles to designate these differences.

Hamilton, the powerful patron of the Gazette, was the theme of its highest panegyric. "He is the highest jewel in Columbia's crown. As a pillar in the Federal building he seems to unite the solidity of the Doric order, the delicacy and elegance of the Ionic, and the towering beauty of the Corinthian." In return for this subserviency, Fenno, as we shall presently see, merely demanded cash.

It was to furnish an antidote to the aristocratic and monarchical sentiments of Fenno's paper that Freneau's "National Gazette" was established, and the better we know the Gazette of the United States, the plainer does it become that an antidote was needed. The columns of Fenno's paper read like those of a journal of the court of St. James. A few paragraphs will illustrate: "The principal ladies of the city have with the earliest attention and respect paid their *devoirs* to the amiable consort of our beloved president, namely, the Lady of his Excellency, the Governor, Lady Stirling, Lady Mary Watts, Lady Kitty Duer, La Marchioness de Breham, the ladies of the Most Honorable Mr. Layton, the Most Honorable Mr. Dalton,

---

* Gazette of the United States, March, 1790.

the Mayoress, Mrs. Livingston of Clermont, Lady Temple, Madam de la Forest, Mrs. Houston, Mrs. Griffin, the Miss Bayards and a great number of other respectable characters."

Again: "We are informed that the President, His Excellency, the Vice-President, His Excellency, the Governor of this State, and many other personages will be present at the theatre this evening."

Again: "The Most Honorable Morris and Lady attended the theatre last evening."

Such royal gibberish as this could not be reasoned with and Freneau did not attempt to reason with it, but he drove it out of Fenno's paper and out of the United States. He caused it to be laughed at, and that it could not endure. A bit of horse-play like the following was far more effective than any amount of abstraction could have been: —The writer, in imagination goes ahead of the time ten years and gives a page of news for the year 1801—

" On Monday last arrived in this city in perfect health, His Most Serene Highness the Protector of the United States, who on Wednesday next will review the regular troops which compose the garrison."

" Yesterday came on before the circuit court of the Protector, the trial of James Barefoot, laborer, for carelessly treading on the great toe of My Lord Ohio. The defendant was found guilty, but as the offense appeared quite accidental, and his lordship had already inflicted on him fifty lashes, the court fined him only 100 pounds and ordered him to be imprisoned six months. Considering the blood and rank of the prosecutor, the humanity of the sentence cannot be too highly extolled. His lordship's toe is in a fair way of recovery, although one of his physicians thinks the nail is in danger."

" Yesterday was capitally convicted by a majority of the jury, John Misprision, for high treason, for lying with the mistress of the Protector's second son, the duke of Erie. Great efforts will be made to obtain a pardon, but it is feared that the enormity of the offense, with a suspicion of its being the third or fourth time he has taken this liberty with his Grace, will prevent their desired effect."

" Sunday last, being the birthday of the Protector's lady, was celebrated in this city with becoming attention. No divine service was performed. The levee of her Highness was remarkably crowded. She looked uncommonly cheerful considering it is the ninth month of her pregnancy. In the evening the theatre was unusually brilliant in expectation of her Highness's company, who for the reason just mentioned was obliged to forego the pleasure."

" It is said that Lady Champlaine, a maid of honor to her Highness the Protectoress, has had an intrigue with the Duchess of Rye's footman."

" To remedy the inconveniences attending the election on the death of every protector, a bill will be brought in at the next session of Congress to make the office hereditary, and to increase his annual revenue from five hundred thousand to one million of dollars. It is certainly impossible for his Highness to support the dignity of his high station upon his present small allowance."

" The hereditary council will meet in the future at the new palace in Philadelphia. This superb edifice cost the moderate sum of six hundred thousand dollars, ten cents and five mills, which exceeded the calculations of the first lord of the Treasury only by two dollars, three cents and one mill."

" A few copies of the act to restrain the freedom of press may be had at this office."

Monarchy was not the only thing the National Gazette abhorred. Freneau, as a life-long democrat and consistent whig, detested the avowed principles of the federal party and there was no love in his heart for its leader, Alexander Hamilton. Hamilton was therefore singled out and made the principal target for the anti-federal arrows that sped from Freneau's bow. It was upon the appearance of Hamilton's report on manufactures that Freneau's career as a publicist began. The Secretary of the Treasury announced the startling doctrine that it was the unquestionable meaning of the constitution that Congress had power to provide for any object that concerned the general welfare. The phrase " general welfare," he contended, was susceptible neither of specification nor of definition. Every object which in its operations extends throughout the union concerns the general welfare and it was left to the discretion of the National Legislature to decide what shall be regarded as concerning the general welfare. The Secretary entertained no doubts that whatever concerned education, agriculture, manufacturing, or commerce was within the sphere of the action of the National Government.

Freneau, as a champion of strict construction, swooped down upon the doctrine of "implied power" with savage talons. "Is there," the Gazette asks, "*any* object for which money is not necessary, or any object for which money may not be applied and brought under the object of congress? Under such a construction of the power of congress, what is to become of the word constitutional? Nothing henceforth would be unconstitutional. It would be the easiest thing in the world to conceive that religion is a matter of the general welfare; and then an ecclesiastical establishment supported by government would quickly follow. Besides, such a doctrine knocks down every boundary worth contending for between the general government and the state government. This doctrine of non-specification and non-limitation of the power of the constitution was subversive of liberty."[30] The Secretary is charged with bad faith in attempting to promulgate such ideas. He is reminded that when he urged the adoption of the constitution, he taught the people that usurpation was not to be apprehended; that construction by implication was impossible, that the states had nothing to fear. Now, by a little refinement in politics, and by the legerdemain of fiscal operations, he was about to do all that he had promised would not and could not be done. The funding scheme, the bank scheme, the excise, were all contrary to himself, the constitution and American freedom.

Hamilton was unfitted by nature to brook opposition, and he met the opposition of Freneau in a most unfortunate manner. At first he left his defense in the hands of his editor Fenno, but Fenno was a heavy fellow and could do little but rave. He hurled invective against any who should dare to criticize a measure of government. The National Gazette, he said was the vehicle of party spleen and the opponent of the principles of order, virtue and religion;[31] its editor was a "wretch," "a spaniel," "a fawn-

[30] National Gazette, 1792.
[31] Gazette of the United States, Aug. 2, 1792.

ing parasite," "a black-guard," "a grumbletonian," "a crack brain," "a Bedlamite," "a jackal of mobocracy," "a salamander." Freneau reprinted in his own paper these courtly epithets, and kept calm. A few lines of doggerel was all the reply he would vouchsafe to his enraged adversary.

Since the day I attempted to print a gazette
This Shylock-Ap-Shenkin does nothing but fret;
Now preaching and screeching, then nibbling and scribbling
Remarking and barking and whining and pining
     And still in a pet,
From morning 'till night with my humble Gazette.

Instead of whole columns our page to abuse,
Your readers would rather be treated with news;
While wars are a-brewing, and kingdoms undoing,
While monarchs are falling, and princesses squalling,
While France is reforming, and Irishmen storming—
In a glare of such splendor, what folly to fret
At so humble a thing as a poet's Gazette.

One Printer for Congress (some think) is enough
To flatter and lie, to palaver and puff,
To preach up in favor of monarchs and titles,
And garters and ribbands to prey on our vitals.

To criticise government and governors seemed to him a perfectly legitimate act and he exercised this right without any great perturbations of conscience. A squib from his paper furnishes the basis of a philosophy for the freedom of press:

" Free government in any country naturally urges by imperceptible advances to tyranny, unless corrected by the vigilance of the people. Nothing but the perpetual jealousy of the governed has ever been found effectual against the machination of ambition. When this jealousy does not exist in some reasonable degree the saddle is soon placed upon the backs of the people and occupied by a succession of tyrants. There never was a government that had not its flatterers whose incense of adulation is always in readiness to be offered at the shrine of power, and whose abilities are prostituted to cover the abuse of office. Monarchies it is well known owe no small share of their disability to such support. Republics ought to be above it." [32]

---

[32] National Gazette, 1791.

But it must not be inferred that Freneau abused the liberty of the press. The National Gazette was not a scurrilous or libellous sheet. It has an unsavory reputation in history, but we shall see before we have finished, that it does not deserve such a reputation, that scurrility and slander are not a feature of its pages. It was called atheistical and subversive of religion and morals, not because it denied the existence of God or attacked religion, for it let such subjects severely alone, but because it advocated democratic principles. In those days if a man was a democrat he was an atheist, and that was all there was to it. Compared with the Daily Advertiser, a republican contemporary, or with Fenno's paper, the National Gazette was a mild and decent sheet. The fear and hatred that it won for itself arose from the ability with which it was edited. It was supported by the best talent of the age. Hugh Brackenridge, Freneau's classmate at college, now eminent as a jurist, sympathized with the aims of the paper and contributed largely to its success by writing for its columns.[*] James Madison worked for it, talked for it, and wrote for it.[**] Jefferson could not have been more interested in it if his political life had depended upon its success. He was always writing about it to his friends, calling attention to its merits, and drumming up subscribers and subscriptions. He kept Freneau supplied with foreign newspapers, and thus enabled him to make his paper the source of the fullest information respecting the mighty movements and triumphs of democracy in Europe. By good management on the part of the

---

[*] Brackenridge, Francis Hopkinson, and Freneau are admitted by critics to be the three greatest American prose writers of the eighteenth century. Freneau's prose writing is characterized by Moses Coit Tyler as "delightful, easy, sinewy, touched with a delicate humor, crisp and keen edged." Lit. Hist. American Revolution, vol. ii, 275.

[**] "I used occasionally to throw in an article with a view chiefly to contrast the monarchical spirit which characterized Fenno's paper." Randall's "Thomas Jefferson," vol. ii, p. 74.

editor and his friends, the paper prospered and became the power it was sought to make it. In May, 1792, Freneau published the following card in his paper: "Upward of six months being elapsed since the publication of this paper, and the subscriptions having succeeded beyond the editor's most sanguine expectations, he now begs leave to solicit the attention of the people of the United States to a publication which he trusts will at all times be found truly republican in its principles and tendency."

The chief business of the Gazette was to destroy Hamilton, the one man in whom the hopes of the federalists lay. That the Secretary of the Treasury was the head and front of the federal party was clearly recognized by Jefferson. "Hamilton is really a colossus to the anti-republicans," he writes to Madison. "Without numbers he is a host within himself. When he comes forward there is nobody but yourself who can meet him. For God's sake take up your pen and give him a fundamental reply." [26] Freneau, after the manner of editors generally, did not concern himself deeply about "fundamental replies." His plan was to render Hamilton and his schemes odious and unpopular. Every utterance, every report, every recommendation of the Secretary was construed as having but one ultimate aim—the overthrow of the constitution and the establishment of a monarchy. His funding system, his national bank, his excise law, his love of titles, his advocacy of a perpetual public debt, his loose-construction notions, were all of the same cloth. If you want rules for the conversion of a limited republic into an absolute monarchy, said Freneau, here they are:

1. Get rid of constitutional shackles.
2. Confer titles of rank. If the principal magistrate should be particularly venerable in the eyes of the people take advantage of that fortunate circumstance.
3. If the principal magistrate is averse to titles, persevere in indoctrinating the people with the idea. Time will gain it respect.

---

[26] Jefferson's Works, vol. iv, p. 122.

4. Harp incessantly upon the dangers of the mob.

5. Let the great nostrum be a perpetual public debt. If a debt is not at hand *assume* one, and then swell it and stretch it in every possible way.

6. Interest the legislators in speculation and speculators in legislation.

7. Establish an incorporated bank by which those who are to inherit the kingdom that is preparing for them may be enriched.

8. Arrogate all power to the general government under the phrase " general welfare."

9. Secure a rich manufacturing class by making laws in their interests.

10. Create a standing army.

11. Take England as a model.

Hamilton's doctrine that a public debt is a public blessing was resisted by the National Gazette with bull-dog ferocity. " Brutus," who fulminated for months against the funding system ably supported these charges:

1. The funding system threw $50,000,000 into the hands of the wealthy.

2. It combined the money interest with the monopoly of the National Bank.

3. By its excise and impost offsprings it swallowed up by future payments the last resource of the country.

4. The certificates of indebtedness fell into the hands of speculators and foreigners.

5. It had diverted capital from its proper channels and turned it into speculation.

6. It created an immense body of revenue officials from the Secretary down to the tide-waiter, all ·bound together by common interests.

The editor's compassion was deeply moved for the soldier of the revolution who had been paid by certificates of indebtedness which had passed out of his hands at a discount into the hands of speculators, and which by Hamilton's law, had appreciated to several times their value. The theme caused the editor to drop into rhyme:

> Public debts are public curses
> In *soldiers'* hands; there nothing worse is!
> In speculators' hands increasing,
> A public debt's a public blessing.

Jonathan Pindar, who is Philip Freneau[*] in disguise, appears before Hamilton and other magnates as candidate for the position of poet-laureate. To further his chances of appointment he promised to swear—

> The nation's debt's a blessing vast,
> Which far and wide its general influence sheds,
> From whence Pactolian streams descend so fast,
> On their—id est—the speculators' heads.

> That to increase this blessing and entail
> To future time its influence benign,
> New loans from foreign nations cannot fail
> While standing armies clinch the grand design.

> That taxes are no burthen to the rich,
> That they alone to labor drive the poor—
> The lazy rogues would neither plow nor ditch,
> Unless to keep the sheriff from the door.

Freneau was a master of irony and frequently subjected Hamilton's sensitive nerves to this species of wit. The following piece is a sample of the fine satire that was constantly directed against the federalists and their chief:

A NEW POLITICAL CREED.

"Whoever would live peaceably in Philadelphia, above all things it is necessary that he hold the federal faith and the federal faith is this, that there are two governing powers in this country, both equal and yet one superior; which faith unless one keep undefiledly without doubt he shall be abused everlastingly. The Briton is superior to the American and the American is superior to the Briton, and yet they are equal and the Briton shall govern the American.

"The Briton while here is commanded to obey the American and yet the American ought to obey the Briton; and yet they ought not both to be obedient. For there is one dominion nominal of the American and another dominion real of the Briton. And yet there are not two dominions but only one dominion.

"The American was created for the Briton and the Briton for the American, and yet the American shall be a slave to the Briton and the Briton the tyrant of the American.

---

[*] Jefferson says these "Probationary leaders," as they were called, were written by St. George Tucker and not by Freneau. They were, at any rate, saddled on the editor. Ford's Writings of Thomas Jefferson, vol. vi, p. 328.

"The Britons are of three denominations, and yet only of one soul, nature, and subsistence: The Irishman of infinite impudence; the Scotchman of cunning most inscrutable; and the Englishman of impertinence altogether insupportable.

"For the true faith is that we believe and confess that the government is fallible, and infallible: Fallible in its republican nature; and infallible in its monarchical tendency; erring in its state individuality and unerring in its federal complexity. So that it is both fallible and infallible; yet it is not twain but one government only, as having consolidated all state dominion in order to rule with sway uncontrolled. This is the true federal faith, which except a man believe and practice faithfully, beyond all doubt he shall be cursed perpetually."

Such reading was exceedingly painful to a proud and highly organized nature like Hamilton's. Fenno defended the Secretary as best he could, but Fenno was no match for Freneau. The National Gazette continued to pour forth its effective broadsides until Hamilton's patience gave way and he determined to break a lance in his own behalf. Freneau he affected to despise. In the editor and clerk who met his eyes daily in the office of government he saw only the servile instrument of Thomas Jefferson. Without evidence and without reason he cherished the notion that the National Gazette had been established by the Secretary of State, and that it was supported and directed by him, and that Freneau was a man of straw. With vision blurred and his facts all tangled, Hamilton rushed into print with an attack upon Jefferson. The chastisement, of course, had to be administered over Freneau's shoulders. In July, 1792, there appeared in Fenno's Gazette the following communication:

Mr. Fenno:

The editor of the National Gazette receives a salary from the government. *Quaere:* Whether this salary is paid for translations or for publications the design of which is to villify those to whom the voice of the people has committed the administration of our public affairs,—to oppose the measures of government and by false insinuation to disturb the public peace?

In common life it is thought ungrateful for a man to bite the hand that puts bread in his mouth, but if the man is hired to do it, the case is altered.   T. L.

"T. L." was Alexander Hamilton. Freneau paid but little attention to the squib, doubtless because he did not suspect its high authority. He re-printed it in his paper and said it was beneath notice, and propounded this query by way of retort: "Whether a man who receives a small stipend for services rendered as French Translator to the Department of State and as editor of a free newspaper admits into his publication impartial strictures on the proceedings of the government, is not more likely to act an honest and disinterested part toward the public than a vile sycophant who, obtaining emoluments from the government far more lucrative than the salary alluded to, finds his interest in attempting to poison the mind of the people by propagating and disseminating principles and sentiments utterly subversive of the true interests of the country and by flattering and recommending every and any measure of government, however pernicious and destructive its tendency might be to the great body of the people?" The world is then called upon to judge between the motives of Freneau and those of Fenno.[37]

The world probably took very little interest in the motives of either of the editors, yet it did take the greatest interest in the names that were soon involved in the controversy that ensued. A struggle between Hamilton and Jefferson was fraught with issues of the most profound significance. The triumph of Hamilton meant conservatism and the rule of the classes in America; the triumph of Jefferson meant radicalism and the rule of the masses. To be precise and just, we may say that Hamiltonism meant a strong central government administered in the English spirit, while Jeffersonism meant a light and easy central government that would respond readily to the will of the populace. Both Jefferson and Hamilton honestly wished to avoid a quarrel, yet a conflict between them was inevitable. Hamilton by a few inopportune strokes of the

---

[37] National Gazette, July, 1792.

pen in a moment of irritation precipitated the contest. In
reply to Freneau's retort he wrote for Fenno's paper, over
the signature "An American," a letter that made peace no
longer possible.

"Mr. Freneau," he said in this letter—thinking and car-
ing nothing about Freneau—"Mr. Freneau should not
escape with the plea that his hostility toward the measures
of government was only a mark of independence and dis-
interestedness." The whole truth in regard to the National
Gazette should be known. That truth for the enlighten-
ment of the world and the discomfiture of Jefferson is then
set forth in these paragraphs:

"Mr. Freneau, before he came to Philadelphia, was employed by Childs and Swaine, printers of the *Daily Advertiser,* in New York, in the capacity of editor or superintendent. A paper more devoted to the views of a certain party,
of which Mr. Jefferson is the head than any to be found
in this city was wanted. Mr. Freneau was thought a fit
instrument; a negotiation was opened with him which
ended in the establishment of the *National Gazette* under
his direction.

"Mr. Freneau came here at once editor of the *National
Gazette* and clerk for foreign languages in the department
of Mr. Jefferson, Secretary of State; an experiment somewhat new in the history of political manœuvres in this
country; *a newspaper instituted by a public officer* and the
editor of it regularly pensioned with the public money in
the disposal of that officer, an example which could not
have been set by the head of any other department without having long since been rung through the United States.
[By the *National Gazette,* of course.]

"Mr. Freneau is not, then, as he would have it supposed, the independent editor of a newspaper who though
receiving a salary from the government has firmness
enough to express its maladministration; he is the faithful and devoted servant of the head of a party from whose
hands he receives the boon. The whole complexion of

this paper exhibits a decisive internal evidence of the influence of that patronage under which he acts. Whether the services rendered are equivalent to the compensation he receives is best known to his employer and himself; there is, however, some room for doubt. It is well known that his employer is himself well acquainted with the French language, the only one of which Mr. Freneau is the translator and it may be a question how often his aid is necessary.

"It is somewhat singular too, that a man acquainted with but one language, engaged in an occupation which it may be presumed demands his whole attention—the editor of a newspaper—should be the person selected as the clerk for foreign languages in the department of the United States for foreign affairs. Could no person be found acquainted with more than one foreign language? and who in so confidential a trust could have been regularly attached to, in the constant employ of the department and immediately under the eye of the head of it?"[*]

Hamilton then turns from Freneau to Jefferson and hauls that gentleman over the coals for divers political iniquities. At the time of Hamilton's attacks, Jefferson was in Virginia designing geometrical wheelbarrows and mould-boards of least resistance. He does not seem to have entered into the *mêlée* but was content to let Freneau and Hamilton fight it out for themselves. Many writers rushed to his defense, but his own hand was stayed, and the hand of Freneau even is not apparent in the replies to Hamilton's attack. Moreover the champions of Jefferson had their articles printed not in the National Gazette but in the Daily Advertiser of Philadelphia.

If the reader has recalled the facts connected with Freneau's coming to Philadelphia he will have seen that Hamilton's charges were nothing more than assumptions. These charges Freneau met in a characteristic way. He

---

[*] Gazette of the United States, Aug., 1792.

went before the Mayor of Philadelphia and, duly swore: "That no negotiation was ever opened with him by Thomas Jefferson, Secretary of State for the establishment or institution of the National Gazette; that the deponent's coming to the city of Philadelphia as a publisher of a newspaper was at no time urged, advised or influenced by the above officer, but that it was his own voluntary act; that the Gazette or the Editor thereof was never directed, controlled or attempted to be influenced in any manner either by the Secretary or any of his friends; that not a line was ever directly or indirectly written, dictated or composed for it by that officer, but that the editor had consulted his own judgment alone in the conducting of it—*free, unfettered and uninfluenced.*" [39]

This solemn and explicit denial by a man whose character was above reproach would have caused a less pertinacious and a more sagacious man than Hamilton to let the matter drop. But his feelings now had the whip hand of his judgment and he could not stop. He rushed further into the blind encounter. He now came forward with the insinuation that Freneau had sworn to a lie. This he said, would be just what a pensioned tool would do. How, he would like to know, was Mr. Freneau able to swear that Mr. Jefferson never wrote a line for his paper. No editor who does not himself write every line for his paper can make any such affirmation as that. Facts were against Mr. Freneau. He then opens his artillery of facts:

" It is a fact, Mr. Freneau, that you receive a salary as clerk for foreign languages, and yet you can translate but one language."

" It is a fact that you left New York to become the editor of the *National Gazette.*"

" It is a fact that your appointment was antecedent to the commencement of your paper." [40]

" It is a fact that Mr. Jefferson was in the beginning opposed to the constitution."

---

[39] Gazette of the United States, Aug., 1792.

[40] Freneau's appointment was made Aug. 3, 1791. The first number of the Gazette appeared Oct. 31, 1791.

" It is a fact that that officer arraigns the principal measures of government."

" From these facts the inferences which are to be drawn are irresistible. If you had previously been the conductor of a newspaper in this city—if your appointment had been any considerable time subsequent to the institution of your paper, there might have been some room for subterfuge. But as matters stand you have no possible escape."

" It makes no difference, Mr. Freneau, whether there was a preliminary negotiation or not; there are many facts to presuppose that such a negotiation did occur, and these facts will be brought out, sir, if scruples of family connection or the dread of party resentment do not forbid. And the evidence adduced will be incontestable. Any honest man must conclude that the relations that subsist between you and Mr. Jefferson are indelicate, unfit, and suspicious. Your apology that the meagre compensation provided renders it necessary for the translator to engage in some other occupation is inadmissible, for a competent clerk could have been employed at a full salary, and if his work as a translator did not occupy all this time, he could have used his surplus time at some other kind of work in the department. If there had been difficulty in finding such a man, undoubtedly, you, the editor of a newspaper should not have been selected, and the fact that you were selected is a proof of sinister design. The fact that your predecessor, Mr. Pintard, received but two hundred and fifty dollars a year and was a newspaper man is not to the point; the employment of that gentleman was a natural consequence of a particular situation. These strictures involve you, Mr. Freneau, but it is confessed that they are aimed at a character of greater importance in the community." [41]

Nothing could be more flimsy and illogical than the above, and it is strange that an intellect like Hamilton's should have expressed itself in such a way. It was due doubtless to the fact that he had begun the controversy in a mental fog and could not find his way out. He had got the cart before the horse. On Aug. 11, 1792, he made the charge that Madison had conducted an unworthy negotiation with Freneau, and two days after wrote to Elias Boudinot for an authentication of the charge. " If I recollect right," Hamilton says to Boudinot, " you told me, that this, if necessary, could be done; and if practicable it is of

[41] Gazette of the United States, Aug., 1792; Hamilton's Works, vol. v, p. 518.

real importance that it should be done. It will confound and put down a man who is continually machinating against public happiness." (Not Freneau but Jefferson is meant.)

" You will oblige me in the most particular manner by obtaining and forwarding to me without delay the particulars of all the steps taken by Mr. Madison—the when and the where—with the liberty to use the name of the informant. His *affidavit* to the facts, if obtainable would be of infinite value."

But behold! " the when and the where " and the " affidavit of infinite value," to meet Freneau's affidavit did not materialize. Boudinot informs him that there is no direct evidence of a negotiation available; that the gentleman upon whom he relied for information was more attached to Freneau than he had supposed and would say nothing; that there was nothing but hearsay upon which to base the charge, although he (Boudinot) would do all he could to get together some evidence." Hamilton also wrote to Jonathan Dayton for " the when and the where " of the alleged negotiation, but that gentleman, although desirous of frustrating the designs of a particular party, could not comply with his request.

Freneau called for the proof that was promised, declining to answer charges of a personal nature unless they were supported by the declarations of persons. But proof there was none, and Hamilton was driven to the miserable confession " that the secret intentions of men being in the **repositories of their own breasts it rarely happens and is therefore not to be expected that direct and positive proof of them can be adduced. *Presumptive facts and circumstances* must afford the evidence."**

After this graceless acknowledgment that his charges against Freneau were without proof, Hamilton spared the

---

" Hamilton's Works, vol. v, p. 520.
" Parton's Life of Jefferson, p. 447.

editor and applied his bad names to Jefferson direct. The bringing of Freneau into this quarrel was most unfortunate to Hamilton's cause and reputation. He stood before the country convicted of an unwarranted attempt to injure an innocent private citizen in order that he might punish a political enemy. And the country did not forgive him. "He lost something," says Parton, "which is of no value to an anonymous writer in a presidential campaign, but is of immense value to a public man—WEIGHT." His query in Fenno's paper calling in question Freneau's honor was the beginning of his political downfall. Besides, viewed from the standpoint of private morality, Hamilton's attack upon Freneau was very low, for he was himself doing precisely what he accused Jefferson of doing. He was supporting a partisan paper by means of the patronage of his department. Freneau did not fail to bring out the fact that Fenno was exclusive printer to the treasury department, and that his emoluments in that direction were twenty-five hundred dollars per annum.[44] And candid history brings out another fact still more damaging, to wit, that Fenno was at times the direct beneficiary of Hamilton's private purse. Not long after the attack upon the editor of the National Gazette, Fenno wrote to Hamilton stating that he was in financial straits and that if the hand of benevolence and patriotism were not speedily extended to him his career as a printer would be over.[45] Hamilton upon the receipt of the letter wrote to his friend Rufus King as follows:

"My Dear Sir:
"Inclosed is a letter just received from poor Fenno. It speaks for itself.
"If you can without delay raise 1000 dollars in New York, I will endeavor to raise another thousand at Phila-

---

[44] National Gazette, Sept., 1793.
[45] Life of Rufus King, vol. x, p. 502.

delphia. If this cannot be done we must lose his services and he will be the victim of his honest public spirit.

"Yours truly,

"A. HAMILTON."

"Poor Fenno" continued to publish his Gazette, hence it is tolerably certain that the "hand of benevolence and patriotism" was in some way extended.

Either a consciousness of his innocence or his stubborn nature prevented Freneau from offering an elaborate defense against Hamilton's charges. His biographer therefore is not called upon to dwell long upon his exculpation. As we have seen, Jefferson kept out of the quarrel. His name as far as possible was kept out of the National Gazette. He was attacked in Fenno's paper and defended in the Daily American Advertiser, a paper which was as violent in its republicanism as Freneau's paper. In one of the articles in the Advertiser in behalf of Jefferson is the following incidental defense of Freneau:

"Mr. Freneau has the following well-authenticated claim for the office of Translator. A native of the Middle States, he had been liberally educated at Princeton. To an accurate knowledge and a refined taste in the English language, he had added a similar acquirement in the French, the nation with whom we have the most intimate relations and whose language has become in a great measure throughout Europe the general medium of political negotiation. Through life his morals were without blemish and his conduct in the revolution was that of a sound whig and republican. Perhaps his sufferings as a prisoner of war may have excited additional sympathy in his favor. [In the matter of getting an appointment.] To what trait in his character, to what defect in his qualification does "American" [Hamilton] object? To his occupation? and if so, to occupations in general or to printing in particular? The low rate of pay made it necessary to get one engaged in some other business. Is printing less honorable, less beneficial to mankind than all others? Does "American" come forward to traduce it and lessen it? Vain and unworthy effort! Whether he had already set up a press or was about to set up one, —for "American" can have it either way—is a matter of indifference. He could not take the clerkship without the aid of the press. The objection in the point of influence, if the characters in question were capable of it, is scarcely worthy of notice. The office was created by law and a salary attached to it. If the person appointed performs these duties, what other claim can the principal have upon him? Degraded indeed would be the condition of a freeman, if an appointment to an office carried with it low subservience to the Superior. It is treasonable to infer that any such subservience exists between a superior and his subordinate and a great injustice has been done both Jefferson and Freneau by ' American.' " [46]

We cannot let the Hamilton-Freneau-Jefferson quarrel drop without giving Jefferson's version of the affair. Washington had called his two secretaries to task for their bickerings and implored them in the name of the country to cease from their strife. Jefferson answered at considerable length the charge that he had set up the National Gazette and that Freneau was his hireling:

" While the government was at New York I was applied to on behalf of Freneau to know if there was any place within my department to which he could be appointed. I answered there were but four clerkships, all of which I found full and continued without any change. When we removed to Philadelphia, Mr. Pintard, the translating clerk, did not choose to remove with us. His office then became vacant. I was again applied to there for Freneau and had no hesitation to promise the clerkship to him. I cannot recollect whether it was at the same time or afterwards, that I was told he had a thought of setting up a paper there." [47] But whether then or afterwards, I considered it a circumstance of some value, as it might enable me to do what I had long wished to have done, that is to have the material parts of the Leyden Gazette brought under your eye, and that of the public, in order to possess yourself and them of a juster view of the affairs of Europe, than could be obtained from any other public source. This I had ineffectually attempted through the press of Mr. Fenno, while in New York, selecting and translating passages myself at first, then having it done by Mr. Pintard, the translating clerk, but they found their way too slowly into Fenno's paper. Mr. Bache essayed it for me in Philadelphia, but his being a daily paper did not circulate sufficiently in other states. He even tried, at my request, the plan of a weekly paper of recapitulation from his daily paper, on hopes it might go into the other States, but in this, too, we failed. Freneau as translating clerk and the

[46] American Daily Advertiser, Oct., 1792.
[47] We cannot gather from the correspondence whether it was before or afterwards. The offer was made Feb. 28, 1791. A letter from Madison, May, 1791, reads as if Jefferson was aware of Freneau's intention.

printer of a periodical paper likely to circulate through the states
(uniting in one person the parts of Pintard and Fenno) revived
my hopes that they could at length be effected. On the establishment of his paper, therefore, I furnished him with the Leyden
Gazettes with an expression of my wish that he could always
translate and publish the material intelligence they contained, and
have continued to furnish them from time to time as regularly as
I have received them. *But as to any other direction or any indica-
tion of my wish how his press should be conducted, what sort of
intelligence he should give, what essays encourage, I can protest in
the presence of Heaven that I never did by myself or any other,
or indirectly say a syllable nor attempt any kind of influence. I can
further protest in the same awful presence, that I never did by
myself or any other, directly or indirectly write, dictate, or procure
any one sentence or sentiment to be inserted in his or any other
gazette, to which my name was not affixed or that of my office.*
I surely need not except here a thing so foreign to the present
subject as a little paragraph about our Algerian captives, which I
once put into Freneau's paper.

"Freneau's proposition to publish a paper having been about
the time that the writings of Publicola and the discourses of
Davila had a good deal excited the public attention, I took for
granted from Freneau's character, which had been marked as that
of a good whig, that he would give free place to pieces written
against the aristocratical and monarchical principles these papers
had inculcated. This having been in my mind, it is likely enough
I may have expressed it in conversation with others, though I do
not recollect that I did. To Freneau I think I could not, because
I still had seen him but once and that was at a public table, at
breakfast at Mrs. Elsworth's, as I passed through New York the
last year. And I can safely declare that my expectations looked
only to the chastisement of the aristocratical and monarchical
writings, and not to any criticism on the proceedings of government. Colonel Hamilton can see no motive for any appointment
but that of making a convenient partizan. But you, sir, who have
received from me recommendations of a Rittenhouse, Barlow,
Paine, will believe that talents and science are sufficient motives
with me in appointments to which they are fitted, and that Freneau
as a man of genius, might find a preference in my eye to be a
translating clerk and make a good title to the little aids I could
give him as the editor of a Gazette by procuring subscriptions to
his paper as I did some before it appeared, and as I have done
with pleasure for other men of genius. Col. Hamilton, alias
' Plain Facts,' says that Freneau's salary began before he resided
in Philadelphia. I do not know what quibble he may have in
reserve on the word ' residence.' He may mean to include under
that idea the removal of his family; for I believe he removed
himself before his family did to Philadelphia. But no act of mine
gave commencement to his salary before he so far took up his

abode in Philadelphia as to be sufficiently in readiness for his duties of his place. As to the merits or demerits of his paper they certainly concern me not. He and Fenno are rivals for the public favor. The one courts them by flattery, the other by censure, and I believe it will be admitted that the one has been as servile as the other severe. No government ought to be without censors; and where the press is free, no one ever will." [48]

This solemn and semi-official history of the establishment of the National Gazette agrees perfectly with the facts as they have hitherto been related in these pages. It agrees with the account given by James Madison,[49] with the sworn statement of Freneau, and it must stand as true history until evidence is produced to shake it. Freneau was the independent editor of an independent paper.

The charge of perjury with which Hamilton tried to blacken Freneau's character, aroused the resentment of the poet and excited the editor to the fullest exercise of his license.[50] If the federalists had heretofore been scourged with whips, they were now scourged with scorpions. Every phase of their policy was assailed in the National Gazette most bitterly, most fearlessly, and with a persistence that was as relentless as fate. The senate held its sessions with closed doors. The Gazette attacked these doors with a crow-bar. Appealing to Hamilton's "great beast"—the people—it says:

A motion for opening the doors of the senate chamber has again been lost by a considerable majority—in defiance of instruction, in defiance of your opinion, in defiance of every principle

---

[48] Writings of Jefferson, vol. vi, pp. 106-108.
[49] Writings of Madison, vol. i, pp. 569-570.
[50] Fenno continued to cast discredit upon Freneau's oath. "Enquirer" wanted to know if Freneau took the oath reverently, if he kissed the holy evangel in a pious manner. The correspondent suspects that instead of kissing the Bible he saluted with reverence a copy of Jefferson's "Notes on Virginia." A doubting rhymester thus delivered himself:

> To many a line in humble prose
> Thy voice is wont to swear,
> And once to shame thy patron's foes
> Didst lie before the mayor.

Gazette of the United States, Aug., 1792.

which gives security to free men. What means this conduct? Which expression does it carry strongest with it, contempt for you or tyranny? Are you freemen who ought to know the individual conduct of your legislators, or are you an inferior order of beings incapable of comprehending the sublimity of senatorial functions, and unworthy to be entrusted with their opinions? How are you to know the just from the unjust steward when they are covered with the mantle of concealment? Can there be any question of legislative import which freemen should not be acquainted with? What are you to expect when stewards of your household refuse to give account of their stewardship? Secrecy is necessary to design and a masque to treachery; honesty shrinks not from the public eye."

" The Peers of America disdain to be seen by vulgar eyes, the music of their voices is harmony only for themselves and must not vibrate in the ravished ear of an ungrateful and unworthy multitude. Is there any congeniality excepting in the administration, between the government of Great Britain and the government of the United States? The Senate supposes there is, and usurps the secret privileges of the House of Lords. Remember, my fellow citizens, that you are still freemen; let it be impressed upon your minds that you depend not upon your representatives but that they depend upon you, and let this truth be ever present to you, that secrecy in your representatives is a worm which will prey and fatten upon the vitals of your liberty."

Freneau could be trusted to keep the " truth ever present " before the mind of the public, and after little more than a year of agitation the doors of the senate were opened to the public and secrecy no longer preyed upon the vitals of liberty. His hostility to Hamilton's National Bank scheme was equally pronounced. To a " Truly Great Man " (Washington) he addresses these lines:

> George, on thy virtues often have I dwelt,
> And still the theme is grateful to mine ear,
> Thy gold let chemists ten times even melt
> From dross and base alloy they'll find it clear.
>
> Yet thou'rt a man—although perhaps, the first,
> But man at best is but a being frail;
> And since with error human nature's curst,
> I marvel not that thou shouldst sometimes fail.
>
> That thou hast long and nobly served the state
> The nation owns, and freely gives thee thanks,
> But, sir, whatever speculators prate,
> She gave thee not the power to establish BANKS.

" National Gazette, Feb., 1792.

Probably to no other influence was the final downfall of the National Bank more directly traceable than to the hatred for it which was inspired in the minds of the people by the National Gazette. Freneau was now the leading editor in America. He was the oracle for all editors of humble democratic sheets. In the south, where there were but few newspapers, it was the only paper that had a general circulation." The leaders of the republican party left no stone unturned to get it among the people, and the fifteen hundred copies of its circulation were sent where they would do the most good. In the small papers of the country extracts from it were published as coming from a sacred source. Examine a democratic paper of the time and the chances are that you will find in it a clipping from the National Gazette and when the extract is found, the chances are still great that it is an attack upon the National Bank." Public opinion was in a formative state when Freneau attacked the bank scheme, and the seeds of enmity to it which he sowed fructified in its destruction.

The strength of the paper, however, is to be found in its democracy and in its perpetual harping upon the theme of federal enmity to republican government and federalist love of monarchy. There may have been no intention in the minds of the federal leaders to abandon republican forms of government as soon as expedient, yet Freneau believed there was and made the people believe there was; and that was all that was necessary for the success of democracy.

Jefferson, as we shall see, could not be induced even by Washington to forsake Freneau, and we are not surprised at his loyalty, for Freneau was a thorough Jeffersonian, and in the Gazette Jefferson's opinions were reflected as in

---

" In Virginia, in 1791, there were nine newspapers; in South Carolina, three; in North Carolina, two; and in Georgia, two. National Gazette, Nov., 1791.

" One of the charges against the Gazette was that it was circulated in every state. National Gazette, March 27, 1792.

● 37

a mirror. We can imagine the pleasure of the great democrat in the little sentiments from Paine and Rousseau which
sparkled in the columns of the Gazette; or this morsel of
an epitaph for the tomb of Frederick the Great:

> Here lies a king, his mortal journey done,
> Through life a tyrant to his fellow-man;
> Who bloody wreaths in bloody battles won—
> Nature's worst savage since the world began.[54]

In January, 1793, "Louis Capet lost his caput"—as the
irreverent Boston Argus put it—and France was declared
a republic. In May of the same year, citizen Genet, the
embassador of the new republic after an almost triumphal
journey northward from Charleston, arrived in the city of
Philadelphia amid the roar of cannon and the acclamations
of a noisy populace. War had just been declared by
France against England and the ebullient minister was
sent by his government to awaken the sympathy and secure the aid of America in behalf of France. His mission
began with the brightest prospect of success. Farmers
and merchants offered him provisions at a lower price
than they would sell them to the agent of any other nation. Six hundred thousand barrels of flour were at his
disposal.[55] When he passed through a city, enthusiastic
lovers of France crowded the avenues shouting for the liberty of the nation that had helped America to secure her
own freedom. At Philadelphia three thousand went out to
Dobb's Ferry to meet the representative of the sister republic; while a counter demonstration, gotten up by the
lovers of England, numbered barely three hundred. Genet
was banqueted on every possible occasion and toasted
sometimes when a toast to Washington was forgotten.
Men put on the tri-colored cockade, joined Jacobin clubs,
and restricted the form of salutation to "citizen."

Citizen Freneau was with the French heart and soul.
The French cause was dear to him for sentimental reasons

---

[54] Freneau's Poems.   [55] National Gazette, May, 1793.

as well as for political, for, as De Lancey says, "although he belonged to the third generation of his family in America, he was as thorough a Frenchman as if he had been born under the sunny skies of Provence or had drawn his first breath amid the Bordelais or beneath the lofty tower of an ancient chateau of historic Normandy."[56] With the warmth of a Frenchman and the boldness of an American he threw the influence of his paper upon the side of the French party. The interests of America became in his mind identical with the interests of France. He believed with John Dickinson that if "France did not succeed in her contest every elective republic upon earth would be annihilated and that the American republic would be crushed at once." As between France and England it was impossible for Freneau's fervid and positive mind to profess neutrality. "When of two nations the one has engaged herself in a ruinous war for us, has spent her blood and money for us, has opened her bosom to us in peace and has received us on a footing almost with her own citizens, while the other has moved heaven and earth and hell to exterminate us in war, has insulted us in all her councils, in peace shut her doors to us in every port where her interest would admit it, libelled us in foreign nations, endeavored to poison them against the reception of our most precious commodities: to place these two nations on an equal footing is to give a great deal more to one than to the other, if the maxim be true that to make unequal quantities equal you must add more to one than to the other. To say in excuse, that gratitude is never to enter into the notions of national conduct is to revive a principle which has been buried for centuries, with its kindred principles of the lawfulness of assassination, perjury and poison."[57] That is the way the matter appeared to Jefferson; Freneau's feelings upon the subject were still stronger.

---

[56] Edward F. De Lancey in Proceedings of the Huguenot Soc.
[57] Jefferson's Works, vol. iii, p. 98.

But the president decided that it was no time for gratitude and declared by proclamation that the United States
should pursue an impartial course and should grant nothing to France that was not granted to England also. A
storm of disapproval burst upon the president's head
when this proclamation was published. Of all the voices
that were lifted up against his policy, none was louder and
none was more distinctly heard by the president or gave
him more discomfiture than the voice of Freneau. "Sir,"
said the editor to the president, "Sir, let not, I beseech
you, the opiate of sycophancy, administered by interested
and designing men, lull you into a fatal lethargy at this
awful moment. Consider that a first magistrate in every
country is no other than a public servant whose conduct
is to be governed by the will of the people." [*]

When Genet had brought upon himself the united opposition of the administration and had alienated many of his
supporters by his high-handed actions and by his boast
that he would appeal from the president to the people,
Freneau stood by him and supported him to the last.
"Why all this outcry," he said, "against Mr. Genet, for
saying he would appeal to the people? Is the president a
consecrated character that an appeal from him must be
considered criminal? What is the legislature of the union
but the people in congress assembled? And is it an
affront to appeal to them? The minister of France, I
hope will act with firmness and with spirit. The people
are his friends, or rather the friends of France, and he will
have nothing to apprehend, for as yet the people are sov-
ereign in the United States. Too much complacency is an
injury done his cause, for as every advantage is already
taken of France (not by the people) further condescension
may lead to further abuse. If one of the leading features
of our government is pusillanimity, when the British lion
shows his teeth, let France and her minister act as becomes

---

[*] National Gazette, June, 1793.

the dignity and justice of their cause and the honor and faith of nations." [58]

This was strong language and it affected Washington powerfully. Before this French interference he had never been crossed in his policy, and criticism went hard with him. "By God," he said in one of those passions that sometimes took possession of him, "By God that he had rather be in his grave than in his present situation. That he had rather be on his farm than to be made emperor of the world; that that rascal Freneau, sent him three copies of his paper every day, as if he thought he would become the distributor of his paper; that he could see nothing in this but an impudent design to insult him." [59]

Washington was so sensitive and fretful upon the subject of Freneau that he intimated to Jefferson that it would be agreeable to him if the secretary would withdraw Freneau's appointment as translating clerk. "But I will not do it," said Jefferson. "His paper has saved our constitution *which was galloping fast into monarchy*, and has been checked by no one means so powerfully as by that paper. It is well and universally known that it has been that paper which has checked the career of the monocrats and the president has not with his usual good sense looked upon the efforts and effects of that free press and seen that though some bad things have passed through it to the public, yet the good have preponderated immensely."

Jefferson could have discharged Freneau but he could not have silenced him. The sturdy editor had taken up the French cause for its own sake and without regard to consequences. His perfect independence in the management of his paper is attested to indirectly by Jefferson in a letter written to Madison after Genet had been abandoned by the more discreet republicans. Speaking of Genet, Jefferson says in this letter: " He has still some defend-

---

[58] National Gazette, July, 1793.
[59] Jefferson's Works, vol. i, p. 231.

ers in Freneau's and Greenleaf's papers. Who they are
I do not know." " This was written after Jefferson had
abandoned Genet. Does the language imply subserviency
upon the part of Freneau? If the National Gazette had
been under the control of Jefferson would it have continued to support a cause after its master had withdrawn
his support from the cause?

Besides being its greatest literary champion, Freneau
was in other ways a conspicuous figure among the pro-
moters of the French cause. His editorial office was a
rendezvous for French sympathizers; he solicited and collected funds to be sent to France, acting as agent for the
" French Society of Patriots of America." " At the not-
able civic feast given in Philadelphia in honor of Genet an
ode in French was read, and Citizen Freneau was requested
to translate it into English. This the poet did in an uncommonly careless and unhappy fashion.

Historians have the habit of abusing Freneau for the
part he played in the French incident and they are espe-
cially severe when they animadvert upon his opposition
to Washington. It is difficult to see why this habit has
not been laid aside. Freneau as a partisan of France had
for company the greatest and wisest of the land, patriots
and statesmen and scientists. The heart of America, its
generosity, its justice, its pride, its gratitude were all on
the side of giving assistance to the French. Policy alone
dictated neutrality. Freneau, knowing nothing of policy,
and failing to appreciate the wisdom of Washington's
course, resisted the government in its effort for neutrality.
Washington as the head of the government could not
escape criticism, and Freneau did not spare him. Yet
Freneau's part in the widespread and violent opposition to
Washington has been grossly misrepresented. After reading the story of the French episode as it is usually told,

" Jefferson's Works, vol. i, p. ——.
" National Gazette, July, 1793.

one would expect to find the National Gazette filled with scandalous and scurrilous attacks upon the president. As a matter of fact one will find there nothing of the kind. There are some pretty sulphurous passages in that paper, and no wonder. There were blows to give as well as blows to take. When Fisher Ames spoke of those who supported the French cause "as salamanders that breathed only in fire, as toads that sucked in no aliment from the earth but its poison, as serpents that lurked in their places the better to concoct their venom," *—when a federalist talked that way about French democrats in America, we can scarcely expect the reply of the democrat to be as gentle as the cooing of a dove. But the savage passages in the National Gazette are not directed against Washington. The most offensive paragraph that can be found in Freneau's paper is, unquestionably, one that comments upon the president's proclamation of neutrality. It reads: "I am aware, sir, that some court satellites may have deceived you with respect to the sentiment of your fellow citizens. The first magistrate of a country whether he be called king or president seldom knows the real state of a nation, particularly if he be so buoyed up by official importance as to think it beneath his dignity to mix occasionally with the people. Let me caution you, sir, to beware that you do not view the state of the public mind at this critical moment through a fallacious medium. Let not the little buzz of the aristocratic few and their contemptible minions of speculators, tories and British emissaries, be mistaken for the exalted and generous voice of the American people." The ugliest and coarsest sentence that Freneau published against Washington is to be found in the paragraph just quoted. It was most certainly not written by Freneau, yet he must be held responsible for it. When it is examined and compared with other pasquinades of the time it must be admitted that its tone was mild and

---

* Fisher Ames' Works, vol. ii.

decent. It is equally mild and decent when compared with
editorial utterances of our own day.

Personally Freneau shared the general regard and reverence for Washington, and he let no opportunity slip for
paying tribute to the great man. If placed together, the
verses written by Freneau in Washington's praise would
make a comfortable little volume. Even when the French
trouble was at its height, he could see the greatness of the
man, for, in June, 1793, when Washington was probably
the most unpopular man in America, the poet forgot his
partisanship far enough to publish in his Gazette a graceful and inspiring ode written in the president's praise.

Yet Freneau did not make an idol of Washington. His
working hypothesis was that the president was a man after
all, and he had but little patience with those who affected
to see in Washington a god. It was the fashion in high
federal circles to twist every anti-federal sentiment or
movement into treason to Washington. "Would to God
this same Washington were in heaven," cried Senator
Maclay, disgusted with what he thought was Washington-
worship. "We would not then have him brought forward
as the constant cover to every unconstitutional and irre-
publican act."* When soon after Washington's death ex-
travagant and even blasphemous encomiums appeared
from every quarter, Freneau thus rebuked their fulsome-
ness:

> One holds you more than mortal kind,
> One holds you all ethereal mind,
> This puts you in your Savior's seat
> That makes you dreadful in retreat.
>
> One says you are become a star,
> One makes you more resplendent far;
> One sings that when to death you bowed
> Old mother nature shrieked aloud.
>
> We grieve to see such pens profane
> The first of chiefs, the first of men;
> To Washington—a man who died—
> Is " Abba, father," well applied!

---

* Maclay's Journal, p. 351.

He was no god, ye flattering knaves,
He " owned no world," he ruled no waves,
But—and exalt it if you can—
He was the upright HONEST MAN.

In the autumn of 1793, Philadelphia was stricken by a
deadly plague. A putrid yellow fever broke out in the
city and thousands of victims perished. Half of the popu-
lation fled into the country. Government offices were
closed and business came to a standstill. In the general
depression that accompanied the pestilence Freneau suffered with others. His list of talents did not include a
talent for business and the finances of his paper were badly
managed. Subscribers though often dunned failed to re-
mit; and it was upon subscriptions that the paper chiefly
depended, for the editor scrupulously refused to allow advertisements to encroach upon the space allotted to reading matter.

On the 26th of October, the following notice was inserted in the Gazette:

With the present number (208) conclude the second volume and
second year's publication of the *National Gazette.* Having just
imported a considerable quantity of new and elegant type from
Europe, it is the editor's intention to resume the publication in a
short time—at the opening of the next congress.
Please send in subscriptions.
☞ Printers of newspapers may no longer send in exchange
until further notice.

About the time of the discontinuance of the newspaper,
Jefferson resigned his office, and Freneau was compelled
to resign his clerkship in the department of state. It is
not absolutely certain that a bankruptcy wound up the
affairs of the Gazette. The yellow fever may have driven
out Freneau as it drove out thousands of others. Jefferson writing to Randolph said: " Freneau's paper is dis-
continued. I fear it is the want of money. I wish the
subscribers in our neighborhood would send in their
money." * In a letter to Wm. Giles, Freneau says: " Sev-

---

* Jefferson's Works, vol. vi, p. 428.

eral unfavorable circumstances have determined me to a final discontinuance of the National Gazette."[*] Precisely what the unfortunate circumstances were we do not know. Three causes for abandoning the Gazette are suggested by the facts: Shortage in subscription money, the prevalence of the yellow fever, and the loss of government patronage and of his clerkship through Jefferson's resignation. The publication of the paper was never resumed. Freneau as an editor had done his work.

What was that work? What was the mission of the National Gazette? What was its influence upon American politics and upon the American mind?

We have considerable material from which we may draw answers to these questions, for politicians have expressed themselves freely regarding the National Gazette. For Hamilton's opinion of the paper we are prepared: "As to the complexion and tendency of that Gazette a reference to itself is sufficient. No man who loves the government or is a friend to tranquility but must reprobate it as an incendiary and pernicious publication."[*] And again: "If you have seen some of the last numbers of the Gazette you will perceive that the plot thickens and that something very like a serious design to subvert the government discloses itself." To Hamilton's mind, then, the Gazette was a most dangerous foe to the government—which happened to be the federalist party.

The testimony of John Adams regarding the influence of Freneau is interesting. "We Federalists," he wrote to Benjamin Stoddard, "are completely and totally routed and defeated. If we had been blessed with common sense we would not have been overthrown by Freneau, Duane, Callendar or their great patron and protector."[*] In a

---

[*] From a letter in the possession of the Pennsylvania Historical Association.
[*] Hamilton's Works. vol. vii, p. 32.
[*] John Adams' Works, vol. viii, p. 514.

letter to Thomas Jefferson,"' Adams says: "What think you of terrorism, Mr. Jefferson? I shall investigate the motive, the incentive to these terrorisms. I shall remind you of Philip Freneau, Lloyd, Ned Church," etc.—naming other partisan writers. Late in life the aged statesman said: "The causes of my retire.aent are to be found in the writings of Freneau, Markoe, Ned Church""'—and other troublesome newspaper men." It will be seen that when Adams begins to name the writers that have injured his political fortunes, he always puts Freneau at the head of the list. The Editor of the National Gazette seems to have lain like an incubus upon his life. For the year 1791 there is but one entry in his diary and that is a jotting respecting the National Gazette. In writing to Tristam Dalton in 1797 Adams says: "I have ever believed in his [Jefferson's] honor, integrity, love of country and friends. I may say to you that his patronage of Paine and Freneau is and has long been a source of inquietude and anxiety to me."" When it assailed Washington, Adams rejoiced, saying that he himself had held the post of libellee-general long enough. The following verses are a sample of the writings that Adams found so destructive of his peace:

TO A WOULD-BE GREAT MAN.
Certat tergeminis tollere honoribus.
Daddy vice, Daddy vice,
One may see in a trice
The drift of your fine publication;
As sure as a gun,
The thing was just done
To secure you—a pretty high station.

Defenses you call
To knock down your wall
And shatter the STATE to the ground, sir,
So thick was your shot,
And hellish fire-hot
They've scarce a whole bone to be found, sir.

"' John Adams' Works, vol. ix, p. 582.
"' John Adams' Works, vol. iii, p. 414.
"' Ford's Writings of Jefferson, vol. vii, p. 108.

When you tell us of kings,
    And such petty things,
Good Mercy! how brilliant your pages!
    So bright in each line
    I vow now you'll shine—
Like—a glow worm to all future ages.

On Davilla's [72] page
    Your Discourses so sage
Democratical numskulls bepuzzle
    With arguments tough
    As white leather or buff,
(The republican Bull-dog to muzzle).

Fisher Ames expressed his view of Freneau's paper as a factor in politics in these words: "The manifestoes of the *National Gazette* indicate a spirit of faction that must soon come to a crisis. Every exertion is made through their (the republicans') Gazette to make the people as furious as themselves." [73]

Timothy Dwight of Hartford, "the Metropolitan see of Federalism," upon reading the Gazette was moved to express himself thus: "Freneau your printer, linguist, etc., is regarded here as a mere incendiary and his paper is a public nuisance." [74]

Oliver Wolcott was not quite so severe but he hits the nail pretty squarely on the head when he said that it was the settled purpose of the National Gazette to destroy the popularity of the leading men of our country. [75]

Rufus King complained that the censures of the National Gazette were creating a dissatisfaction with the government. [76]

Freneau's friends have not placed on record as much evidence of the great influence of the Gazette as his enemies have left; yet they have not been silent. We have already seen that Jefferson estimated the Gazette as being

---

[72] Adams' Discourses of Davilla—a treatise defending strong government.

[73] Fisher Ames' Works, vol. i, p. 128.

[74] Gibbs' Washington's and Adams' Administration, vol. i, p. 109.

[75] Ibid.   [76] Life and Correspondence of Rufus King.

one of the strongest influences in American politics. In his judgment, it was the Gazette that saved the United States from drifting into monarchy. The great democrat watched the paper with an anxious eye and its success brought him the highest satisfaction. " Freneau's paper," he wrote to a friend, " is getting into Massachusetts under the patronage of Hancock and Samuel Adams, and Mr. Ames the colossus of the monocrats, will either be left out or have a hard run. The people of that state are republican, but hitherto they have heard nothing but the hymns and lauds of Fenno." [17]

James Madison was also gratified at the work which his old friend was doing in the cause of democracy. " Freneau's paper," he said, " justifies the expectations of his friends and merits the diffusive circulation they have endeavored to procure it." [18]

From the contemporaries of the National Gazette, we may glean some matter that will enable us to form a judgment as to the part it played in the propaganda of democratic doctrine. In the unfriendly Connecticut Courant we find this tribute to its influence: " From the National Gazette whence in streams pure and smoking like a drain from a whiskey distillery it is conveyed to reservoirs established in every part of the community." [19]

In the friendly Independent Chronicle, of Boston, we read: " As the friends of civil liberty wish at all time to be acquainted with every question which appears to regard the public weal, a great number of gentlemen in this and neighboring towns have subscribed for Mr. Freneau's National Gazette." [20]

The Halifax Journal of North Carolina attributes the defeat of Mr. Adams in that state to the discussion of his career in the columns of Freneau's paper. The South

---

[17] Jefferson's Works, vol. iii, p. 491.
[18] Madison's Works, vol. iv, p. 543.
[19] Connecticut Courant, 1792.
[20] Boston Independent Chronicle, 1793.

Carolina Gazette was so enraged by Freneau's opposition to the measures of government that it called for his punishment.

These utterances of friends and foes ought to give us a fairly correct notion of Freneau's place in the history of our politics. They teach us that he was hated and feared as the greatest editor of the democratic party. His paper was published in the seed-time of democracy in America. The soil of party politics was virgin and Freneau sowed with a lavish hand. To the federalist mind it seemed that the seeds he was sowing were dragons' teeth which would one day spring up as giants and destroy society and government. Society and government were not injured by the principles advocated by the editor, but the federalist party was.

The part Freneau played in the making of democratic sentiment may be summed up as follows:

1. He was the ablest champion of what is known as "Jeffersonian simplicity." The war which he waged upon titles, distinctions, and court-like ceremonies was successful and decisive.

2. Through his paper the strongest opposition to Hamilton's centralizing schemes found expression. If Freneau had not early checked Fenno, it may be that loose construction would have run away with the constitution.

3. Freneau's paper did much to give a French coloring to our political philosophy. The doctrines of liberty, fraternity, equality, of equal rights to all and special privileges to none, was unwelcome to many American minds in Freneau's day, yet this was the keynote of all Freneau's writings. The editor of the National Gazette was the schoolmaster who drilled Jeffersonian or French Democracy into the minds—willing or unwilling—of the American people.

Freneau's place in the history of journalism is distinct and eminent. He is the prototype of the partisan editor.

A recent student of the history of American journalism thus speaks of him:

" Next to Washington, Jefferson and Hamilton, one figure assumes a prominence superior to that of all others engaged in the political contest, not so much perhaps by the weight of his intellect as by his versatility and vivacity and the keenness and the readiness of the weapons he brought to the contest. We refer to Philip Freneau. What Tyrtaeus was to the Spartan was Freneau to the republicans or anti-federalists. In all the history of American letters or of the United States press there is no figure more interesting or remarkable, no career more versatile and varied than that of Philip Freneau." [a]

---

[a] **Magazine of American History, vol. xvii, p. 121.**

CHAPTER IV

THE POET OF THE WAR OF 1812

Freneau had just entered his forties when he ceased to publish the National Gazette. He had given two of the best years of his life to that paper, but there was a long span still before him. Immediately upon leaving Philadelphia he went to Charleston, South Carolina, to visit his brother Peter. Peter Freneau was a democratic editor of repute, the Secretary of State of South Carolina, and Jefferson's political manager in that state. Philip was well received in Charleston and he made friendships while there which were genuine and lasting.

After a pleasant sojourn of several months in the South, Freneau returned to his New Jersey home. There he spent a year or two doing nothing of importance, unless it was to write an occasional attack upon the government and print it in Bache's "Aurora,"—just to let John Adams know that Philip Freneau was still living. With letters in his pocket from Jefferson and Madison recommending him for "his sound discretion and extensive information" the editor applied for the managership of a projected newspaper in New York, but nothing came of that scheme.[1] We may remember that when he closed up the affairs of the National Gazette he had on hand "a considerable quantity of new and elegant type." This type he seems to have removed to his old home in Mount Pleasant, near Middletown Point (now Mattawan), New Jersey, where he set up as a practical country printer. Following the bent of his genius he tried journalism again, this time in the rôle of a country editor. May 2, 1795, he printed

---

[1] Hudson's History of Journalism, p. 187.

the first number of the "Jersey Chronicle." A copy of
this quaint journal is preserved in the library of the New
York Historical Society. It is a little typographical failure, in the form of a quarto, precisely seven inches by eight.

Freneau made his bow to his rural constituents in these
lines: "The Editor in the publication of this paper pro-
poses among other things to present his readers with a
complete history of the foreign and domestic events of the
times, together with such essays, remarks, and observa-
tions as shall tend to illustrate the politics or mark the
general character of the age and country in which we live."
We learn also from the paper that P. Freneau was ready
and willing to print Handbills and Advertisements at the
shortest notice, and upon the most reasonable terms. The
political tone of the Chronicle was of course democratic,
and the editor never failed to deal an opportune blow at
the political aspirations of John Adams and Alexander
Hamilton.

But the chronicle did not prosper. "Newspapers,"
says Hudson, "have not made their mark in New Jersey as
in many of the old states. Situated between New York
and Philadelphia, it has been placed in a position to enjoy
the news facilities of those two cities."[1] After a year of
struggle the editor announced the discontinuance of the
paper, embracing the opportunity "to return his sincere
thanks to such persons as had favored him with their subscriptions and had by their punctuality enabled him to
issue a free, independent and republican paper."

Another literary venture of 1795 was more successful.
Having collected all his poems he published such as he
deemed worthy in an octavo volume at his own press.
The motley type that greets the eye in this interesting volume was probably set by the poet's own hands. This is
the most important edition of Freneau's poetical works
that we have. It contains nearly three hundred poems
written in almost every variety of metre and is "a treasury

---

[1] Hudson's Journalism in the United States, p. 187.

38

of song, tale, satire, epigram and description." In this leather-bound, worm-eaten volume is to be found nearly all that is good, as well as nearly all that is inferior in Freneau. The inferior forms the larger part of the book, to be sure, but there is enough genuine poetry scattered through the volume to keep it utterly from perishing. His volume of 1787 has been deemed worthy of being reprinted in recent years; the volume of 1795 is still more worthy of being rescued from oblivion.

Freneau was not at all disheartened by the failure of the Chronicle. He had lived all his life amid the wreck of newspapers, and for one to go down was to him the most natural thing in the world. Hardly had the little rustic sheet succumbed than he tried his luck again. In March, 1797, in the city of New York, he offered to the reading public the first number of his "Time-Piece and Literary Companion."

This paper was to be a " vehicle for the diffusion of literary knowledge, news, and liberal amusement in general." At first Freneau associated with him as printer one A. Menut, a Canadian. Menut in a short time dropped out and M. L. Davis, a democratic politician of some importance, took his place. Freneau and Davis managed (or mismanaged) the paper until March, 1798, when Freneau withdrew and left Davis the sole manager. Davis kept the paper going until August, 1798, when the Time-Piece went the way of the other ventures.

The Time-Piece is an interesting *potpourri* of literary performances, ranging from discussions upon the cultivation of pumpkins, to schemes for the reorganization of society upon principles of natural right. The political sentiments of the paper were of the purest Jeffersonian quality. It declared for rotation in office, pure and frequent elections, a free church, a free press, and the abolition of entails. As one turns over the leaves of this rare file one cannot but praise the versatility and tact of the editor in catering to the public taste.

When the yellow fever broke out in Philadelphia, Fre-

neau had removed his family to his old home in Mount
Pleasant where a portion of his inheritance still remained
to him. In this quiet village (the name of which, by the
way has recently been changed to Freneau) the poet, when
not upon the sea, spent most of the remaining years of his
life. In his retirement his literary activity did not cease.
The magazines of the day welcomed his poetry and he
contributed to them constantly. Among those occasional
pieces we find one upon the death of Washington. It is
a gracious tribute, and bespeaks magnanimity and large-
heartedness; for the truth is, Freneau had no reason to
love Washington. The country, however, had reason to
love its great chief, and Freneau sang the songs of his
country.

As a publicist he still couched a lance for the republican party. His political pieces generally appeared in
Bache's Aurora, the political successor of the National Gazette. In 1799, he collected a few of these productions
and had them printed in a small octavo volume under the
title: "Letters on Various Interesting and Important
Subjects, many of which have appeared in the Aurora.
Corrected and Much Enlarged. By Robert Slender, O. S.
M."

O. S. M., being interpreted, is, "One of the Swinish
Multitude." These essays were very spicy and some of
them illustrate excellently Freneau's method of striking at
a political enemy. For instance, here is one which shows
how he went about making life unpleasant for John Adams,
and incidentally damaging the chances of the second president for a second term:

The Epitaph of Jonathan Robbins.[*]
(Robert Slender, *Loquitur.*)

I have just seen the end of Robbins, poor, brave, injured, betrayed, unfortunate Robbins. I have seen him

---

[*] This Robbins was a sailor who was delivered up to the English
by the order of an American court, and was hanged on the charge
of inciting mutiny on board the English frigate *Hermione.*
Robbins claimed to be an American citizen, and much political
capital was made out of the episode.

with my "minds eye" as Hamlet says, and a horrid spectacle it was. I have just been composing his epitaph, that will go down to posterity on the faithful and impartial page of history. Here it is:

Reader
If thou be a Christian and a Freeman,
consider
by what unexampled causes
It has been necessary to construct
This monument
of national degradation
and
Individual injustice;
which is erected
To THE MEMORY of a Citizen of the United States,
JONATHAN ROBBINS, MARINER,
A native of Danbury, in the pious and industrious state of
Connecticut:
who
Under the PRESIDENCY OF JOHN ADAMS,
And by his advice,
Timothy Pickering being Secretary of State,
Was delivered up to the British government,
By whom he was ignominiously put to death;
because,
Though an American Citizen,
He was barbarously forced into the service of his country's
worst enemy
and compelled to fight
Against his conscience and his country's good
On board the British frigate Hermione
Commanded by a monster of the name of Pigot.
He
Bravely asserted his rights to freedom as a man and boldly
Extricated himself from the bondage of his tyrannical
Oppressors
After devoting them to merited destruction.
If you are a seaman
Pause:—
Cast your eyes into your soul and ask
If you had been as Robbins was
What would you have done?
What ought you not to do?
And look at Robbins
Hanging at a British yard-arm!
He was your comrade—
And as true a tar as ever strapped a block:
He was your fellow-citizen,
And as brave a heart as bled at Lexington or Trenton.

Like you
He was a member of a Republic
Proud of past glories
and
Boastful of national honor, virtue, and independence.
Like him
You may one day be trussed up to satiate British vengeance,
Your heinous crime
daring to prefer danger or death
To a base bondage—
Alas, poor Robbins!
Alas, poor Liberty!
Alas, my Country!

In the following we see Freneau as a campaign swash-buckler:

OYEZ!!!

" Robert Slender, to the aristocrat, the democrat, the would-be noble, ex-noble, the snug farmer, the lowly plebeian, the bishops and clergy, reverend and right reverend, doctors, and V. O. M.'s little men or title men, gentlemen and simple men, laymen and draymen, and all other men except hangmen (to whom he hath an aversion) throughout this great and flourishing STATE sendeth greeting:

" Whereas a great and important day draweth near in which you are to exercise a great right, no less than to choose, elect, set apart, solemnly dedicate, appoint and highly honor either Thomas McKean, chief judge of Pennsylvania, or James Ross, practitioner at law, with the high sounding title, power and authority of Governor of the State—Having thrown off his apron, laid aside his tools, and neglected for a small time the honorable and ancient employment of shoe-mending, he hath an account of the great division, dissension and contradiction that exists, the fictions, lies, stories, calumnies, misinterpretations, wrong interpretations, assertions and computations, thought proper not to address one of you but all of you, to call upon you in the most solemn manner; to be upon your guard, to open your ears and attend to even a mender of shoes.

" Ye aristocrats and great men, whether merchants, doctors, proctors or lawyers, who sigh for greatness and long for dominion, whose hearts yearn for the glory of a crown, the splendor of a court, or the sweet marrow bones that are to be picked in his majesty's kitchen, whose eyes ache painfully once again to see the stars, crosses, crescents, coronets, with all the hieroglyphical, enigmatical, emblematical and all the other cals including rascals, which adorn the courts of kings—give a strong, true and decided vote for James Ross, who supports, approves, hopes for, longs for, and sighs for all these.

" Ye bishops and clergy, adorers of the triple crown, the mitre, the sable, the high seat in civil power, the much longed for and established church and the ancient and profligate thing called tithes unite your forces, set Christianity at a defiance and give a firm vote for James Ross.

" Ye old tories and refugees, British spies, speculators, guides and pensioners, approvers of British policy, aimers and designers, who in your hearts wish again to crouch under the protecting paw of the British lion—arrange your forces and give a fair vote for James Ross.—He is your sincere friend.

" Ye, supporters of the British treaty, alien bill, stamp act, excise, standing army, funding system, who believe that a public debt is a public blessing, who say that republicanism is anything or nothing, and maintain that treaties made under the sanction of the Constitution are superior to it—draw near—be not idle on the day of election, support James Ross; he thinks as ye do, acts as you act, and will follow where you lead.

" Ye democrats, soldiers of '76, ye supporters of our independence, ye quellers of Great Britain, ye Americans in heart and in hand draw near, remember that Thomas McKean is your brother, the firm freeman, and the real christian—give him your vote.

" Ye free-born Americans, whose hearts beat high for liberty and independence, who fear not the threats and disdain the power of all the tyrants on earth, assert your rights, make known that ye have not forgotten the late struggle, that the mean devices and shallow arguments of the X Y and Z's of the present day are not able to trick you out of your liberty or to make you the tools of a foreign despot—vote for Thomas McKean—the constant asserter of your rights and liberties.

" Ye honest, ye independent, ye virtuous farmers, who sincerely wish to support that unequalled and glorious instrument, the Constitution of the United States, untarnished and unadulterated that ye may have it whole and entire, a sacred deposit to posterity, your best interest is at stake, join not with that troop but give an honest vote for Thomas McKean, the asserter, the supporter and defender of the invaluable rights of his country.

" Ye honest and industrious mechanics who daily sweat for the support of your families, who in the hour of danger are ever found foremost in the ranks to defend your own and your country's rights, vote for Thomas McKean, whom great men cannot make wink at injustice and oppression.

" Let Porcupine growl, Liston pet, the long list of English agents, speculators, approvers of the fate of Jonathan Robbins, tories and refugees, gnash their teeth in vain; be true to your country, proof against bribery, true to posterity, true to yourselves, arrange ye under the banner of freedom and once more conquer, let the word be LIBERTY and McKEAN!"

Freneau promised that if this volume should prove successful another would follow, but no such encouragement followed. When these pieces came out in the Aurora they were interesting, but they were of a day. The volume seems to have fallen flat and a second collection of Mr. Robert Slender's Essays did not appear.

Write and edit and reprint as much as he would, Freneau could not get a living out of literature. To provide for his family the poet again went down to the sea and, about the year 1799, became the captain of a merchantman. For seven or eight years from this date it is hard to keep trace of him. It is only from poems commemorative of scenes or events upon his voyages that we are enabled to get an occasional glimpse of him. In 1801, he was on the island of St. Thomas, and two years later upon the island of Madeira. While strolling around in the elegant shades of Madeira, Freneau, coming up with the god Bacchus, Prince of Madeira, straightway indited him an ode:

> I met him with awe, but no symptoms of fear,
> As I roved by his mountains and springs,
> When he said with a sneer, " How dare you come here
> You hater of despots and kings?"

> " Haste away with your barque on the foam of the main,
> To Charleston, I bid you repair;
> There drink your Jamaica that maddens the brain,
> You shall have no Madeira, I swear.'

But Freneau conciliated the god and sampling some of his choicest wines heaped upon him and them unstinted praise. As Freneau grew older his praise for Bacchus mounted higher and was sounded oftener. When a poet dwells fondly on this theme, one suspects that he is taking too much to strong drink. There is a reason to think Freneau was no exception to the rule.

In 1804, Captain Freneau sailed to the Canary Islands. While upon Teneriffe, he was invited to visit a celebrated nunnery there. He declined the invitation in verse. Thus we may see that a stretch of years was passed upon the deep, sailing sometimes from New York, sometimes from

Charleston to the West Indies and the remote islands of the Atlantic.

In 1807 the poet-captain abandoned his vocation as a sailor never to resume it.[4] On a return voyage, as he approached the heights of Navesink behind which a few miles away lay his home, a longing for retirement seized upon him.

> Proud heights with pain so often seen,
> (With joy beheld once more)
> On your firm base I take my stand
> Tenacious of the shore.
> Let those who pant for wealth or fame
> Pursue the watery road.
> Soft sleep and ease, blest days and nights,
> And health attend these favorite heights,
> Retirement's blest abode.

In a letter to Jefferson written in 1815 he thus writes of his retirement: "Since my last return from the Canary Islands in 1807 to Charleston and from thence to New York with my brigantine Washington, quitting the bustle and distraction of active life, my walks have been confined, with now and then a short excursion, to the neighborhood of Navesink Hills and under some old hereditary trees and on some fields which I well recollect for sixty years. During the last seven years my pen could not be entirely idle and for amusement only now and then I had recourse to my old habits of scribbling verse."

Freneau was fifty-five years of age when he withdrew from serious occupation. Hitherto his life had been one uninterrupted storm; henceforth it was to be one long calm. It is a pleasant picture which he draws of himself in his quiet home.

> Happy the man who safe on shore,
> Now trims at home his evening fire;
> Unmoved he hears the tempests roar,
> That on the tufted groves expire.

---

[4] Jefferson's MS. in Archives of State Department at Washington.
[5] Jefferson's MSS. in Archives of the State Department at Washington.

Although politics and the sea were forsaken, Freneau remained faithful to his muse. His ruling passion was strong to the last. No passing event worthy of commemoration was allowed to go unsung. In 1809 he prepared for the press a fourth edition of his poems, the work appearing in two volumes neatly printed with striking cuts for frontispieces.

"These poems," the author tells us, "were intended to expose to vice and treason their hideous deformity; to depict virtue, honor and patriotism in their natural beauty. To his countrymen in the Revolution, to Republicans and the rising generation who are attached to their sentiments and principles, the writer hopes this collection will not prove unacceptable." The book was gotten out on the strength of a subscription and in the first volume are printed the names of the subscribers. The subscription plan was set a-going by the publishers without the author's knowledge or approbation. Thomas Jefferson subscribed for ten volumes. In Jefferson's letter to Freneau promising a subscription, he says: "I subscribe with pleasure to the publication of your volume of poems. I anticipate the same pleasure from them which the perusal of those heretofore published has given me. . . . . Under the shade of a tree one of your volumes will be a pleasant pocket companion. Wishing you all possible success and happiness, I salute you with constant esteem and respect." James Madison, then president, also subscribed for ten volumes. The popularity of the poet seems to have been greatest in Pennsylvania. In Philadelphia a bookseller subscribed for 200 copies; in Lancaster a dealer engaged to take 150 copies. A host of subscribers came from South Carolina where the name of Freneau was held in high esteem. In all, about one thousand copies were taken by subscription. We must not despise this small number. Looked at in its relation to the number of

---

Jefferson's MS. in Archives of the State Department at Washington.

people, it is as large as an edition of ten or fifteen thousand copies to-day would be. What poet of our time can do better with his fourth edition?

The edition of 1809 is neither so picturesque nor so valuable as the edition of 1795. Many of the poems of the earlier volume have been crowded out for the later performances, and rarely has there been any gain by the substitution. Nevertheless in the six hundred pages of the two volumes there was more good poetry than any American writer had yet produced, for in 1809, be it remembered Longfellow was but two years old, Poe and Holmes were infants, Bryant had just entered his teens and Lowell was not yet born.

The clash of arms that announced for the second time American resistance to British aggression was a signal for the old poet to tune his harp anew. As he had been the poet of the Revolution so now he became the poet of the war of 1812. Nothing throughout his life gave him more pleasure than to extol his countrymen at the expense of England. It was the poet's way of indulging hatred. He followed closely the progress of the second war and many a ballad from his pen celebrated the glory of our armies upon land and upon sea. His pieces, we are told, were held in great favor by sailors, and were for many years reprinted in broadsides and sold at all our ports.[7] In 1815, he collected most of these martial performances and printed them in two small volumes at the press of David Longworth, of New York city. On the title page of this rare and forgotten edition the poet thus bids defiance to England:[8]

> Then England come! a sense of wrong requires
> To meet with thirteen stars your thousand fires,
> Through these stern times the conflict to maintain,
> Or drown them with your commerce in the main.

---

[7] Griswold's American Poets, p. 34.
[8] The title is: A collection of Poems on American Affairs, and a variety of other subjects chiefly moral and political. By Philip Freneau.

The theme of the first poem of these volumes of his old age is the theme of his life—democracy. In the opening lines we recognize the philosophy of Jefferson and the policy of Madison:

> Left to himself, where'er man is found,
> In *peace* he aims to walk life's little round,
> In peace to sail, in peace to till the soil,
> Nor force false grandeur from a brother's toil;
> All but the base, designing, scheming few
> Who seize on nations with a robber's view,
> These, these with armies, navies potent grown,
> Impoverish man and bid the nation moan;
> These with pretended balances of state
> Keep worlds at variance, breed eternal hate,
> Make man the poor, base slave of low design,
> Degrade the nature to its last decline,
> Shed hell's worst blots on his exalted race,
> And make them fear, and mean to make them base.

The following stanzas were written when England had about reached the end of her tether in her policy of terrorizing American commerce and when war was about to be declared. They are bad from the critic's point of view, but there is a ring and a movement about them which is distinctly bellicose and which must have been taking with those who wanted to fight.

> Americans! rouse at the rumors of war
> Which now are distracting the hearts of the nation,
> A flame blowing up to extinguish your power,
> And leave you a prey to another invasion;
> A second invasion as bad as the old,
> When, northward or southward wherever they strolled,
> With heart and with hand, a murdering band,
> Of vagrants come over to ravage your land;
> For liberty's guard you are ever arrayed,
> And know how to fight in sun or in shade.
>
> Remember the cause that induced you to rise,
> When oppression advanced with her king making boast,
> 'Twas the cause of our nation that bade you despise,
> And drive to destruction all England's proud host,
> Who with musket and sword, under men they adored,
> Rushed into each village and rifled each shade,
> To murder the planter and ravish the maid.

All true-born Americans join as of old
For Freedom's defense be your firm resolution;
Whoever invades you by force or by gold,
Alike is a foe to 'a free constitution;
Unite to pull down that imposture, a crown,
Oppose it, at least, 'tis a mark of the beast,
All tyranny's engines again are at work
To make you as poor and as base as the Turk.

After the best is said, it must be confessed that Freneau's last work was his worst. The edition of 1815, like most of his poetry, consisted chiefly of occasional pieces and it is the usual fate of occasional pieces to be speedily forgotten. The volume was reviewed in the "Analectic Magazine"—a New York periodical—in a kindly tone. "A considerable part of the present collection," wrote the critic, "relates to the transactions of the late war and scarcely a memorable incident either on land or water has escaped the glance of his ever-vigilant and indefatigable muse. He depicts land and naval fights with much animation and gay coloring, and being himself a son of old Neptune, he is never at a loss for appropriate circumstances and expressive dictum when the scene lies at sea. His martial and political ballads are free from bombast and affectation and often have an arch simplicity of manner that renders them striking and poignant. The strains of Freneau are calculated to impart patriotic impulses to the hearts of his countrymen and their effect in this way should be taken as a test of their merit." [*]

With the war of 1812 and the appearance of the poems just noticed, Freneau's career as a writer ended. A short poem under his name may now and then be found in the magazines and newspapers up almost to the time of his death, but writing was no longer a serious business with him. His last years were spent in rural retirement in his New Jersey home. He was, however, far from being a recluse. New York was easily accessible by boat and he frequently visited the scenes of his better days. He could

---

Analectic Magazine, 1815.

not forget his old democratic friends and they do not seem
to have forgotten him. Jefferson, when president, is said
to have remembered him with special favor. The story
goes that Jefferson sent to Freneau asking him to come to
Washington on important business, and that the poet replied in these words: "Tell Thomas Jefferson that he
knows where Philip Freneau lives and if he has important
business with him let him come to Philip Freneau's house
and transact it." This bumptiousness (if Freneau was
really guilty of using these words), did not alienate Jefferson, for later he tendered the poet an office under the government. The position was declined."

In New York literary circles he was affectionately received as the "Veteran Bard of the Revolution." We
have a charming account of the personal life of the poet
in his old age, written by one who knew him well. The
sketch is rambling and somewhat garrulous, yet it is so
graphic that it must be quoted at length:" "Freneau was
widely known to a large circle of our most prominent and
patriotic New Yorkers. His native city, with all his wan-
derings, was ever uppermost in his mind and affections.
. . . . . He was esteemed a true patriot, and his private
worth, his courteous manner and his general bearing won
admiration with all parties. His pen was more acri-
monious than his heart. He was tolerant, frank in expression, and not deficient in geniality. He was highly culti-
vated in classical knowledge, abounding in anecdotes of
the revolutionary crisis, and extensively acquainted with
prominent characters.

"It was easy to record a long list of eminent citizens who
ever gave him a cordial welcome. He was received with
the warmest greetings by the old soldier, Governor George

" New Bedford Mercury, 1884.
" The quotation is from the pen of Dr. J. W. Francis, a former
president of the New York Historical Society. It was written at
the request of E. A. Duyckinck, who wished it for his article on
Freneau in his Cyclopedia of American Literature.

Clinton. He also found agreeable pastime with the learned Provoost, the first regularly consecrated Bishop of the American Protestant Episcopate, who himself shouldered a musket in the revolution and hence was called the fighting Bishop. They were allied by classical tastes, a love of natural science and ardor in the cause of liberty. With Gates he compared the achievements of Monmouth with those of Saratoga; with Col. Fish he reviewed the capture of Yorktown; with Dr. Mitchell he rehearsed from his own sad experience the physical sufferings and various diseases of the incarcerated patriots of the Jersey prison-ship; and descanted on Italian Poetry and the piscatory eclogues of Sannazius. He, doubtless, furnished Dr. Benjamin De Witt with data for his funeral discourse on the remains of the 11,500 American Martyrs. With Pintard he could laud Horace and talk largely of Jones; with Sylvanus Miller he compared notes on the political clubs of 1795-1810. He shared Paine's vision of an ideal democracy.

"I had when very young read the poetry of Freneau and as we instinctively become attached to the writers who first captivate our imaginations, it was with much zest that I formed a personal acquaintance with the revolutionary bard. He was at that time about seventy-six years old when he first introduced himself into my library. I gave him a hearty welcome.

"New York, the city of his birth, was his most intimate theme; his collegiate career with Madison, next. His story of many of his occasional poems was quite romantic. As he had at command types and a printing-press, when an incident of moment in the Revolution occurred he would retire for composition or find shelter under the shade of some tree, indite his lyric, repair to the press, set up his types, and issue his productions. There was no difficulty in versification with him. I told him what I had heard Jeffrey, the Scotch Reviewer say of his writings, that the time would arrive when his poetry like that of Hudibras, would command a commentator like Gray.

" It is remarkable how Freneau preserved the acquisitions of his early classical studies, notwithstanding he had for many years in the after portion of his life been occupied in pursuits so entirely alien to books.

" There is no portrait " of the patriot Freneau; he always declined the painter's art and could brook no counterfeit presentment."

Nearly twenty years of life after his work was over, were left to the poet in which he might mingle with old associates and discuss the past. It is regrettable that the discussion was too often conducted at the tavern over the flowing bowl. When the old bard looked back upon the road he had travelled, he saw it rough and stony; when he looked forward to the little journey that remained, the prospect was still barren and forbidding. His once ample estate had nearly slipped out of his hands. The records of the county court tell of sales of portions of the land of Philip Freneau and of foreclosures of mortgages upon his property."

A short time after the war of 1812, while the poet and his family were at church, his house at Mount Pleasant was burned and all his correspondence and unpublished writings were consumed. One cannot help wishing that the letters he had received from Madison and Jefferson might have been saved. Freneau, reduced now almost to poverty, removed his family to a farm-house situated about two and a half miles from the village of Freehold. This house was occupied by the poet until his death. It still stands as a reminder of his worst days, when

> " The joys of wine are all his boast;
> These for a moment damped his pain,
> The gleam is o'er, the charm is lost,
> And darkness clouds the soul again." "

" The portrait as usually given of Freneau is not genuine. It was sketched by an artist at the suggestion and according to the representation of members of the poet's family. It is pronounced by those who knew the original to be a fair visualization of the man as he appeared at maturity of life. Poems of the Revolution, p. xxxi.

" Records of Monmouth County Court, 1823, 1826. " Freneau.

One stormy night in December, 1832, the old man left Freehold to walk to his home. " He crossed a bog-meadow to shorten the distance. The blinding snow bewildered him and he lost his way and sank in the morass. He succeeded in getting out and gaining dry ground, but in attempting to climb a fence he fell and broke his hip. When discovered he was lying under an apple-tree at the edge of the meadow—dead." [15]

About two hundred yards from the spot where Freneau lived in Mount Pleasant is a neat monument bearing this inscription:

POET'S GRAVE.

PHILIP FRENEAU,

Died Dec. 18, 1832.

Age 80 years, 11 months, 16 days.

He was a native of New York, but for many years a resident of Philadelphia and New Jersey.

His upright and benevolent character is the memory of many and will remain when this inscription is no longer legible.

" Heaven lifts its everlasting portals high
And bids the pure in heart behold their God."

---

[15] New Bedford Mercury, 1884. De Lancey suggests that Freneau was caught in a " blizzard," and it is likely that he was, for the New York paper of Dec. 18, 1832, contains an account of a violent snow storm. See Albany Daily Advertiser, Dec. 18, 1832.

CHAPTER V

CONCLUSION

We may fitly close this sketch by looking over Freneau's career and making an estimate of his personal character. It is important to do this, for a just conception of Freneau's character must be entertained before a nice judgment upon some points in our political history can be rendered.

In its outward aspects Freneau's life was a failure. As a man of genius he availed himself of the undisputed privilege of that class to be unsuccessful in pecuniary matters. It was the fashion for our revolutionary heroes to languish in jail for debt and to die forgotten and penniless. Freneau's lifeless corpse under the apple-tree reminds us of the sad fate of Robert Morris and Charles Henry Lee and Joel Barlow. The poet inherited a comfortable fortune, but this was dissipated long before his death. For many years he lived from hand to mouth. We have seen that he was intemperate. This was also a privilege in Freneau's day, denied to no one, whether to poet or to preacher. Notwithstanding these shortcomings, we do not find that Freneau was a bankrupt either in character or in reputation. On the contrary we have positive evidence that his manhood was sound. James Madison speaks of his "spotless integrity." His publishers have nothing but praise for his worth as a gentleman and a scholar. His friends in New York remembered him as tolerant, polished and genial.[1] A lady who was a neighbor of Freneau and who frequently visited his house told me (in 1898) that his uprightness and honesty were never called into

[1] Encyclopedia of American Literature, vol. i, p. 333.

question. "He died universally loved and regretted by all who knew him," was the tribute of his old friend John Pintard.[2] The sturdiness of his nature was illustrated in the management of the National Gazette. After his great patron Jefferson had abandoned the cause of the French, Freneau with characteristic imprudence and independence, continued to pour his broadsides into the friends of neutrality.

In matters of religion Freneau was indifferent. He subscribed outwardly to orthodox forms, not because he thought they were true, but because he thought they were useful. He was steeped in the philosophy of Rousseau and Condorcet. For the human mind as well as for human institutions he demanded the utmost freedom.

> " Oh, impotent and vile as vain
> They who would the native thought restrain!
> As soon might they arrest the storm,
> Or take from fire the power to warm,
> As man compel by dint of might
> Old darkness to prefer to light.

> " No, leave the mind unchained and free
> And what they ought mankind will be;
> No hypocrite, no lurking fiend,
> No artist, to some evil end,
> But good and great, benign and just
> As God and nature made them first.[3]

Like many other poets from David to our own time, Freneau was a pantheist.

> " All that we see, above, abroad,
> What is it all but nature's God? "

Like that of many poets, it may be added—like that, for instance of Addison or of Steele—his religion was of very little consequence to himself or to any one else. Nevertheless, he tells us that it extended to "a practice of the golden rule, as far as weak nature would permit."[4]

[2] New York Mirror, January, 1833.
[3] Freneau's Poems, 1815 edition.
[4] Essays, Robert Slender, p. 49.

For the austerities of life he had too much contempt. **His** impatience with puritanism finds an expression in **the following** verses on "The Puritans":

> On Sunday their faces were dark as a cloud,
> The road to their meeting was only allowed,
> And those they caught rambling on business or pleasure
> Were sent to the stocks to repent at their leisure.
>
> This day was the mournfullest day in the week;
> Except in religion none ventured to speak.
> This day was the day to examine their lives,
> To clear off old scores and preach to their wives.
>
> In the school of oppression though woefully taught,
> 'Twas only to be the oppressors they sought;
> All, all but themselves were bedevilled and blind,
> And their narrow-souled creed was to serve all mankind.
>
> This beautiful system of nature below,
> They neither considered or wanted to know;
> And called it a dog-house wherein they were pent—
> Unworthy themselves and their mighty descent.

Such writing as this brought upon Freneau the wrath of his New England contemporaries, and earned for him much unwarranted abuse. In Connecticut and Massachusetts the newspapers of his day referred to him as an atheist and the foe of good government, and fame has transmitted this opinion of the man to our own times. Yet there is nothing in the history of Freneau's life to justify such an unfavorable judgment. He was a man of strong conviction and strong utterance and many suffered from the freedom of his lance. A careful examination of his long life, however, reveals nothing in him that was base or low.

With this knowledge of the man's character we are prepared to take up a story that has thrown discredit upon his name and upon the name of Jefferson. The story is that Freneau in his old age said that Jefferson *did* write for the National Gazette; that, indeed, he wrote the most offensive articles that appeared in that paper. In other words, we are told that Freneau admitted that he had

sworn to a lie when he swore before the Mayor of Philadelphia that Jefferson never wrote a line directly, or indirectly, for the Gazette. This is the way the story comes
down to us: Griswold, an encyclopedia maker, said that
Dr. John W. Francis said that Freneau told him that Jefferson wrote for the Gazette. This statement if true would
make both Freneau and Jefferson the clumsiest of liars.
From the nature of the story it cannot be absolutely dis-
proved, but there are strong considerations for not accept-
ing it.

In the first place, Griswold is extremely unreliable. It
is not meant that the learned preacher would deliberately
put into print what he knew to be false, but it is meant
that he was shockingly careless about getting things right.
In illustration of this we may take the first page of the
first edition (1842) of the "Poets and Poetry of America,"
where he attempts to sketch Freneau's life. It would be
difficult to find a page more pregnant with mistakes and
misinformation than this. In one paragraph of four sen-
tences there are five palpable errors. This may be cited
as a curiosity of ignorance:

"As a reward for the ability and patriotism he had dis-
played during the war, Mr. Jefferson gave him (Freneau)
a place in the Department of State; but his public employment being of too sedentary a description for a man of
his ardent temperament he soon relinquished it to conduct in Philadelphia a paper entitled 'The Freeman's Journal.' He was the only editor who remained at his post
during the prevalence of the yellow fever in that city in
1791. The Journal was unprofitable and he gave it up in
1793 to take command of a merchant ship in which he
made several voyages to Madeira, the West Indies and
other places. His naval ballads and other poems relating
to the sea written in this period are among the most spirited and carefully finished of his productions."

Now, (1) Freneau did *not* give up his government position to edit a paper, (2) he did *not* edit the *Freeman's Jour-*

nal, (3) yellow fever was *not* prevalent in Philadelphia in
1791, (4) he did *not* take command of a merchant ship
when he left Philadelphia in 1793, (5) his naval ballads
were *not* composed in the period of which he is speaking.
It is submitted that we should be very reluctant to attach
any importance to anything that such a careless writer
might rehearse from memory.

In the second place, we know that the same Dr. Francis
who is quoted as having cast such a foul imputation upon
Freneau's character, regarded the poet as a man of sterling
integrity. If Freneau had really admitted that he had committed perjury, Francis would hardly have written these
words of the perjurer: " His private worth won the admiration of both parties." Besides, if Freneau had made
such an admission, Dr. Francis, the President of a great
Historical Association would have appreciated its historical significance and would have himself spoken of it in his
sketch of Freneau. In that sketch he does not refer to
any such conversation as Griswold reports.

In the last place, Freneau's whole life is a denial of Griswold's statement. The patriot poet was nothing if not
straightforward and truthful, and our credulity is strained
when we are asked to believe that he deliberately confessed
that he was the greatest of liars and the basest of knaves.
History is wholly against the supposition that Jefferson
ever wrote a line for the National Gazette and there is
not the slightest reason to believe that Freneau ever said
that he wrote for it.

As to Freneau's part in the history of our politics, little
need be added to what has already been said. He was
not a statesman in any sense of the word. A violent temperament and an intolerant nature unfitted him for the
leadership of men, while narrowness of mind made him
unsafe as a counsellor. Nor was he a politician in a practical sense. He sought no office and he entered into no
combinations to secure party advantage. He did not look
to office as a reward for his services as a publicist. He

advocated democracy for its own sake.   In the enthusiasm
born of sincerity of purpose is to be found his greatest
strength.   The glow of conviction was upon all his writings, and when he came out with an article denouncing
Adams or Hamilton, his words burned themselves into
the mind of the public.   He appealed to the populace, who
read and applauded, and when election time came voted his
way.   So sure and so uniform was his success in this field
that it is safe to say that, excepting Jefferson himself,
democracy in America in the first years of our national life
had no abler champion than Philip Freneau.

THE PUBLICATIONS OF PHILIP FRENEAU

(A) Newspapers.

1. "The National Gazette." Published at Philadelphia. First number, October, 1791; last number, October, 1793. A complete file of this paper may be found in the collections of the Library Company of Philadelphia.[1] It is difficult to find a complete file elsewhere.

2. "The Jersey Chronicle." Published in Mount Pleasant, New Jersey, in 1795. A file may be found in the library of the New York Historical Society.

3. "The Time-Piece and Literary Companion." Begun March, 1797. Freneau was connected with it less than a year. A file may be found in the Lennox Library in New York.

(B) Books.

1. "A Poem on the Rising Glory of America; being an Exercise Delivered at the Public Commencement at Nassau Hall, September 25, 1771."

This was published at Philadelphia in 1772. It is a small unbound octavo of 27 pages. It may be found in the Library of Princeton College.

Hildeburn has the following note on this publication:

"It is attributed to Judge H. H. Brackenridge and also to Brackenridge and Freneau jointly. In the Edition of Freneau's Poems, printed on his own press and under his supervision at Monmouth in 1809 [he should have said 1795] this poem is given a prominent place without any reference being made to Brackenridge's share in its composition. On the title page of Brackenridge's 'Poem on Divine Revelation' that piece is said to be by the same person who on a similar occasion *delivered* a small poem on the rising glory of America. This may have been the ground

---

[1] Philadelphia offers the best facilities for the study of Freneau. The Library of the Pennsylvania Historical Society contains nearly all his works.

on which the last-named poem was attributed to Brackenridge. But as it admits of the construction that he only read or recited the earlier poem of which Freneau claims the sole authorship, I have placed it under the latter's name." Hildeburn's Issues of the Press of Pennsylvania, vol. ii, p. 148.

2. "Voyage to Boston. A Poem." A small octavo of 24 pages; printed in Philadelphia in 1775.

3. "The British Prison-Ship A Poem in Four Cantoes." An octavo of 23 pages; printed in Philadelphia in 1781.

4. "New Travels through North America." This is a translation by Freneau of Claude C. Robin's "Voyage dans L'Amerique Septentrionale." This small octavo volume of 112 pages was published in Philadelphia in 1783. It may be found in the library of the Historical Society of Pennsylvania.

5. "The Poems of Philip Freneau, Written Chiefly during the Late War." An octavo volume of 415 pages, published in Philadelphia in the year 1786. This very rare and valuable volume may be found in the Library of the Pennsylvania Historical Society.

6. "A Journey from Philadelphia to New York by way of Burlington and South Amboy. By Robert Slender, Stocking Weaver (Freneau)." This is a small octavo of 28 pages; published in Philadelphia in 1787. It may be found in the New York Historical Library.

7. "The Miscellaneous Works of Mr. Philip Freneau containing his Essays and Additional Poems." Published in Philadelphia, 1788; it may be found in the Library of Congress.

8. "The Village Merchant ": A Poem to which is added the Country Printer. A small octavo of 16 pages, printed at Philadelphia in 1794.

9. "Poems Written between the years 1768 and 1794 by Philip Freneau of New Jersey." This was printed at Mount Pleasant in 1795, at the press of the author. It may be found in the Library of Congress, and in the libraries of Harvard and Columbia Universities. This edition contains the major part of Freneau's poems.

10. "Letters on Various and Interesting Subjects many of which have appeared in the Aurora. By Robert Slender, O. S. M." (O. S. M. = One of the Swinish Multitude.) Small octavo of 142 pages. Published in Philadelphia in 1799. It may be found in the library of the Pennsylvania Historical Society.

11. "A Laughable Poem on Robert Slender's Journey from Philadelphia to New York." This is a reprint under a new title of No. 6.

12. "Poems Written and Published during the American Revolutionary War, and now Republished from the Original Manuscripts interspersed with Translations from the Ancients, and other pieces not heretofore in print." Published in two duodecimo volumes in Philadelphia in 1809. It is to be found in the library of the Pennsylvania Historical Society.

13. "A Collection of Poems on American Affairs, written between the year 1797 and the Present Time." Published in New York in two duodecimo volumes in 1815. To be found in the Boston Public Library and in the Library of Congress.

14. "Poems on Various Subjects, but chiefly illustrative of the Events and Actors in the American War of Independence." This is a reprint of the edition of 1786. It was published in *fac-simile* in London in 1861 by J. R. Smith.

15. "Poems Relating to the American Revolution." With an Introduction, Memoir, and Notes by E. A. Duyckinck, New York, 1865.

16. "Some Account of the Capture of the Ship Aurora." New York, 1899.